THE TRAGICAL HISTORY OF DOCTOR FAUSTUS FROM THE QUARTO OF 1604

THE TRAGICAL HISTORY OF DOCTOR FAUSTUS FROM THE QUARTO OF 1604

Christopher Marlowe

www.General-Books.net

Publication Data:

Title: The Tragical History of Doctor Faustus From the Quarto of 1604
Author: Marlowe, Christopher, 1564-1593
Reprinted: 2010, General Books, Memphis, Tennessee, USA
Subjects: Germany – Drama
Bisac subject codes: DRA000000, DRA003000, DRA010000, LIT004120, LIT013000, LIT015000,

How We Made This Book for You
We made this book exclusively for you using patented Print on Demand technology.
First we scanned the original rare book using a robot which automatically flipped and photographed each page.
We automated the typing, proof reading and design of this book using Optical Character Recognition (OCR) software on the scanned copy. That let us keep your cost as low as possible.
If a book is very old, worn and the type is faded, this can result in numerous typos or missing text. This is also why our books don't have illustrations; the OCR software can't distinguish between an illustration and a smudge.
We understand how annoying typos, missing text or illustrations, foot notes in the text or an index that doesn't work, can be. That's why we provide a free digital copy of most books exactly as they were originally published. You can also use this PDF edition to read the book on the go. Simply go to our website (www.general-books.net) to check availability. And we provide a free trial membership in our book club so you can get free copies of other editions or related books.
OCR is not a perfect solution but we feel it's more important to make books available for a low price than not at all. So we warn readers on our website and in the descriptions we provide to book sellers that our books don't have illustrations and may have numerous typos or missing text. We also provide excerpts from books to book sellers and on our website so you can preview the quality of the book before buying it.
If you would prefer that we manually type, proof read and design your book so that it's perfect, simply contact us for the cost. Since many of our books only sell one or two copies a year, unlike mass market books we have to split the production costs between those one or two buyers.

THE TRAGICAL HISTORY OF DOCTOR FAUSTUS FROM THE QUARTO OF 1604

THE TRAGICAL HISTORY
OF
DOCTOR FAUSTUS
  By Christopher Marlowe
From The Quarto of 1604
  Edited by The Rev. Alexander Dyce
  DRAMATIS PERSONAE.
  THE TRAGICAL HISTORY OF DOCTOR FAUSTUS
  FOOTNOTES
  THE TRAGICALL HISTORY OF D. FAUSTUS. AS IT HATH BENE ACTED BY THE RIGHT HONORABLE THE EARLE OF NOTTINGHAM HIS SERUANTS. WRITTEN BY CH. MARL.

    In reprinting this edition, I have here and there amended the text by means of the later 4tos,–1616, 1624, 1631.–Of 4to 1663, which contains various comparatively modern alterations and additions, I have made no use.
    DRAMATIS PERSONAE.
THE POPE.
CARDINAL OF LORRAIN.

THE EMPEROR OF GERMANY.
DUKE OF VANHOLT.
FAUSTUS.
VALDES,] friends to FAUSTUS.
CORNELIUS,]
WAGNER, servant to FAUSTUS.
Clown.
ROBIN.
RALPH.
Vintner.
Horse-courser.
A Knight.
An Old Man.
Scholars, Friars, and Attendants.
DUCHESS OF VANHOLT
LUCIFER.
BELZEBUB.
MEPHISTOPHILIS.
Good Angel.
Evil Angel.
The Seven Deadly Sins.
Devils.
Spirits in the shapes of ALEXANDER THE GREAT, of his Paramour
and of HELEN.
Chorus.

THE TRAGICAL HISTORY OF DOCTOR FAUSTUS
FROM THE QUARTO OF 1604.

Enter CHORUS.

CHORUS. Not marching now in fields of Thrasymene,
Where Mars did mate1 the Carthaginians;
Nor sporting in the dalliance of love,
In courts of kings where state is overturn'd;
Nor in the pomp of proud audacious deeds,
Intends our Muse to vaunt2 her3 heavenly verse:
Only this, gentlemen,–we must perform
The form of Faustus' fortunes, good or bad:
To patient judgments we appeal our plaud,
And speak for Faustus in his infancy.
Now is he born, his parents base of stock,
In Germany, within a town call'd Rhodes:
Of riper years, to Wertenberg he went,
Whereas4 his kinsmen chiefly brought him up.
So soon he profits in divinity,
The fruitful plot of scholarism grac'd,
That shortly he was grac'd with doctor's name,

Excelling all whose sweet delight disputes
In heavenly matters of theology;
Till swoln with cunning,5 of a self-conceit,
His waxen wings did mount above his reach,
And, melting, heavens conspir'd his overthrow;
For, falling to a devilish exercise,
And glutted now6 with learning's golden gifts,
He surfeits upon cursed necromancy;
Nothing so sweet as magic is to him,
Which he prefers before his chiefest bliss:
And this the man that in his study sits.
      it.

FAUSTUS discovered in his study.7
FAUSTUS. Settle thy studies, Faustus, and begin
To sound the depth of that thou wilt profess:
Having commenc'd, be a divine in shew,
Yet level at the end of every art,
And live and die in Aristotle's works.
Sweet Analytics, 'tis thou8 hast ravish'd me!
Bene disserere est finis logices.
Is, to dispute well, logic's chiefest end?
Affords this art no greater miracle?
Then read no more; thou hast attain'd that9 end:
A greater subject fitteth Faustus' wit:
Bid Economy10 farewell, and11 Galen come,
Seeing, Ubi desinit philosophus, ibi incipit medicus:
Be a physician, Faustus; heap up gold,
And be eterniz'd for some wondrous cure:
Summum bonum medicinae sanitas,
The end of physic is our body's health.
Why, Faustus, hast thou not attain'd that end?
Is not thy common talk found aphorisms?
Are not thy bills hung up as monuments,
Whereby whole cities have escap'd the plague,
And thousand desperate maladies been eas'd?
Yet art thou still but Faustus, and a man.
Couldst12 thou make men13 to live eternally,
Or, being dead, raise them to life again,
Then this profession were to be esteem'd.
Physic, farewell! Where is Justinian?
      Reads.

Si una eademque res legatur14 duobus, alter rem,
alter valorem rei, c.
A pretty case of paltry legacies!

Reads.

Exhoereditare filium non potest pater, nisi, c.15
Such is the subject of the institute,
And universal body of the law:16
This17 study fits a mercenary drudge,
Who aims at nothing but external trash;
Too servile18 and illiberal for me.
When all is done, divinity is best:
Jerome's Bible, Faustus; view it well.
 Reads.

Stipendium peccati mors est.
Ha!
Stipendium, c.
The reward of sin is death: that's hard.
 Reads.

Si peccasse negamus, fallimur, et nulla est in nobis veritas;
If we say that we have no sin, we deceive ourselves, and
there's no truth in us. Why, then, belike we must sin, and so
consequently die:
Ay, we must die an everlasting death.
What doctrine call you this, Che sera, sera,19
What will be, shall be? Divinity, adieu!
These metaphysics of magicians,
And necromantic books are heavenly;
Lines, circles, scenes,20 letters, and characters;
Ay, these are those that Faustus most desires.
O, what a world of profit and delight,
Of power, of honour, of omnipotence,
Is promis'd to the studious artizan!
All things that move between the quiet poles
Shall be at my command: emperors and kings
Are but obeyed in their several provinces,
Nor can they raise the wind, or rend the clouds;
But his dominion that exceeds in this,
Stretcheth as far as doth the mind of man;
A sound magician is a mighty god:
Here, Faustus, tire21 thy brains to gain a deity.
Enter WAGNER.22
Wagner, commend me to my dearest friends,
The German Valdes and Cornelius;
Request them earnestly to visit me.
WAGNER. I will, sir.
 it.

FAUSTUS. Their conference will be a greater help to me
Than all my labours, plod I ne'er so fast.
Enter GOOD ANGEL and EVIL ANGEL.
GOOD ANGEL. O, Faustus, lay that damned book aside,
And gaze not on it, lest it tempt thy soul,
And heap God's heavy wrath upon thy head!
Read, read the Scriptures:—that is blasphemy.
EVIL ANGEL. Go forward, Faustus, in that famous art
Wherein all Nature's treasure23 is contain'd:
Be thou on earth as Jove24 is in the sky,
Lord and commander of these elements.25
    eunt Angels.

FAUSTUS. How am I glutted with conceit of this!
Shall I make spirits fetch me what I please,
Resolve26 me of all ambiguities,
Perform what desperate enterprise I will?
I'll have them fly to India for gold,
Ransack the ocean for orient pearl,
And search all corners of the new-found world
For pleasant fruits and princely delicates;
I'll have them read me strange philosophy,
And tell the secrets of all foreign kings;
I'll have them wall all Germany with brass,
And make swift Rhine circle fair Wertenberg;
I'll have them fill the public schools with silk,27
Wherewith the students shall be bravely clad;
I'll levy soldiers with the coin they bring,
And chase the Prince of Parma from our land,
And reign sole king of all the28 provinces;
Yea, stranger engines for the brunt of war,
Than was the fiery keel at Antwerp's bridge,29
I'll make my servile spirits to invent.
Enter VALDES and CORNELIUS.
Come, German Valdes, and Cornelius,
And make me blest with your sage conference.
Valdes, sweet Valdes, and Cornelius,
Know that your words have won me at the last
To practice magic and concealed arts:
Yet not your words only,30 but mine own fantasy,
That will receive no object; for my head
But ruminates on necromantic skill.
Philosophy is odious and obscure;
Both law and physic are for petty wits;

Divinity is basest of the three,
Unpleasant, harsh, contemptible, and vile:31
'Tis magic, magic, that hath ravish'd me.
Then, gentle friends, aid me in this attempt;
And I, that have with concise syllogisms32
Gravell'd the pastors of the German church,
And made the flowering pride of Wertenberg
Swarm to my problems, as the infernal spirits
On sweet Musaeus when he came to hell,
Will be as cunning33 as Agrippa34 was,
Whose shadow35 made all Europe honour him.
VALDES. Faustus, these books, thy wit, and our experience,
Shall make all nations to canonize us.
As Indian Moors obey their Spanish lords,
So shall the spirits36 of every element
Be always serviceable to us three;
Like lions shall they guard us when we please;
Like Almain rutters37 with their horsemen's staves,
Or Lapland giants, trotting by our sides;
Sometimes like women, or unwedded maids,
Shadowing more beauty in their airy brows
Than have the38 white breasts of the queen of love:
From39 Venice shall they drag huge argosies,
And from America the golden fleece
That yearly stuffs old Philip's treasury;
If learned Faustus will be resolute.
FAUSTUS. Valdes, as resolute am I in this
As thou to live: therefore object it not.
CORNELIUS. The miracles that magic will perform
Will make thee vow to study nothing else.
He that is grounded in astrology,
Enrich'd with tongues, well seen in40 minerals,
Hath all the principles magic doth require:
Then doubt not, Faustus, but to be renowm'd,41
And more frequented for this mystery
Than heretofore the Delphian oracle.
The spirits tell me they can dry the sea,
And fetch the treasure of all foreign wrecks,
Ay, all the wealth that our forefathers hid
Within the massy entrails of the earth:
Then tell me, Faustus, what shall we three want?
FAUSTUS. Nothing, Cornelius. O, this cheers my soul!
Come, shew me some demonstrations magical,
That I may conjure in some lusty grove,
And have these joys in full possession.

VALDES. Then haste thee to some solitary grove,
And bear wise Bacon's and Albertus'42 works,
The Hebrew Psalter, and New Testament;
And whatsoever else is requisite
We will inform thee ere our conference cease.
CORNELIUS. Valdes, first let him know the words of art;
And then, all other ceremonies learn'd,
Faustus may try his cunning43 by himself.
VALDES. First I'll instruct thee in the rudiments,
And then wilt thou be perfecter than I.
FAUSTUS. Then come and dine with me, and, after meat,
We'll canvass every quiddity thereof;
For, ere I sleep, I'll try what I can do:
This night I'll conjure, though I die therefore.
 eunt.

Enter two SCHOLARS.44
FIRST SCHOLAR. I wonder what's become of Faustus, that was wont
to make our schools ring with sic probo.
SECOND SCHOLAR. That shall we know, for see, here comes his boy.
Enter WAGNER.
FIRST SCHOLAR. How now, sirrah! where's thy master?
WAGNER. God in heaven knows.
SECOND SCHOLAR. Why, dost not thou know?
WAGNER. Yes, I know; but that follows not.
FIRST SCHOLAR. Go to, sirrah! leave your jesting, and tell us
where he is.
WAGNER. That follows not necessary by force of argument, that you,
being licentiates, should stand upon:45 therefore acknowledge
your error, and be attentive.
SECOND SCHOLAR. Why, didst thou not say thou knewest?
WAGNER. Have you any witness on't?
FIRST SCHOLAR. Yes, sirrah, I heard you.
WAGNER. Ask my fellow if I be a thief.
SECOND SCHOLAR. Well, you will not tell us?
WAGNER. Yes, sir, I will tell you: yet, if you were not dunces,
you would never ask me such a question; for is not he corpus
naturale? and is not that mobile? then wherefore should you
ask me such a question? But that I am by nature phlegmatic,
slow to wrath, and prone to lechery (to love, I would say),
it were not for you to come within forty foot of the place
of execution, although I do not doubt to see you both hanged
the next sessions. Thus having triumphed over you, I will set
my countenance like a precisian, and begin to speak thus:–
Truly, my dear brethren, my master is within at dinner,

with Valdes and Cornelius, as this wine, if it could speak,
would46 inform your worships: and so, the Lord bless you,
preserve you, and keep you, my dear brethren, my dear brethren!47
   it.

FIRST SCHOLAR. Nay, then, I fear he is fallen into that damned art
for which they two are infamous through the world.
SECOND SCHOLAR. Were he a stranger, and not allied to me, yet should
I grieve for him. But, come, let us go and inform the Rector,
and see if he by his grave counsel can reclaim him.
FIRST SCHOLAR. O, but I fear me nothing can reclaim him!
SECOND SCHOLAR. Yet let us try what we can do.
   eunt.

Enter FAUSTUS to conjure.48
FAUSTUS. Now that the gloomy shadow of the earth,
Longing to view Orion's drizzling look,
Leaps from th' antartic world unto the sky,
And dims the welkin with her pitchy breath,
Faustus, begin thine incantations,
And try if devils will obey thy hest,
Seeing thou hast pray'd and sacrific'd to them.
Within this circle is Jehovah's name,
Forward and backward anagrammatiz'd,49
Th' abbreviated50 names of holy saints,
Figures of every adjunct to the heavens,
And characters of signs and erring51 stars,
By which the spirits are enforc'd to rise:
Then fear not, Faustus, but be resolute,
And try the uttermost magic can perform.–
Sint mihi dei Acherontis propitii! Valeat numen triplex Jehovoe!
Ignei, aerii, aquatani spiritus, salvete! Orientis princeps
Belzebub, inferni ardentis monarcha, et Demogorgon, propitiamus
vos, ut appareat et surgat Mephistophilis, quod tumeraris:52
per Jehovam, Gehennam, et consecratam aquam quam nunc spargo,
signumque crucis quod nunc facio, et per vota nostra, ipse nunc
surgat nobis dicatus53 Mephistophilis!
Enter MEPHISTOPHILIS.
I charge thee to return, and change thy shape;
Thou art too ugly to attend on me:
Go, and return an old Franciscan friar;
That holy shape becomes a devil best.
   it MEPHISTOPHILIS.

I see there's virtue in my heavenly words:
Who would not be proficient in this art?

How pliant is this Mephistophilis,
Full of obedience and humility!
Such is the force of magic and my spells:
No, Faustus, thou art conjuror laureat,
That canst command great Mephistophilis:
Quin regis Mephistophilis fratris imagine.
Re-enter MEPHISTOPHILIS like a Franciscan friar.54
MEPHIST. Now, Faustus, what wouldst thou have me do?
FAUSTUS. I charge thee wait upon me whilst I live,
To do whatever Faustus shall command,
Be it to make the moon drop from her sphere,
Or the ocean to overwhelm the world.
MEPHIST. I am a servant to great Lucifer,
And may not follow thee without his leave:
No more than he commands must we perform.
FAUSTUS. Did not he charge thee to appear to me?
MEPHIST. No, I came hither55 of mine own accord.
FAUSTUS. Did not my conjuring speeches raise thee? speak.
MEPHIST. That was the cause, but yet per accidens;56
For, when we hear one rack the name of God,
Abjure the Scriptures and his Saviour Christ,
We fly, in hope to get his glorious soul;
Nor will we come, unless he use such means
Whereby he is in danger to be damn'd.
Therefore the shortest cut for conjuring
Is stoutly to abjure the Trinity,
And pray devoutly to the prince of hell.
FAUSTUS. So Faustus hath
Already done; and holds this principle,
There is no chief but only Belzebub;
To whom Faustus doth dedicate himself.
This word "damnation" terrifies not him,
For he confounds hell in Elysium:
His ghost be with the old philosophers!
But, leaving these vain trifles of men's souls,
Tell me what is that Lucifer thy lord?
MEPHIST. Arch-regent and commander of all spirits.
FAUSTUS. Was not that Lucifer an angel once?
MEPHIST. Yes, Faustus, and most dearly lov'd of God.
FAUSTUS. How comes it, then, that he is prince of devils?
MEPHIST. O, by aspiring pride and insolence;
For which God threw him from the face of heaven.
FAUSTUS. And what are you that live with Lucifer?
MEPHIST. Unhappy spirits that fell with Lucifer,
Conspir'd against our God with Lucifer,

And are for ever damn'd with Lucifer.
FAUSTUS. Where are you damn'd?
MEPHIST. In hell.
FAUSTUS. How comes it, then, that thou art out of hell?
MEPHIST. Why, this is hell, nor am I out of it:57
Think'st thou that I, who saw the face of God,
And tasted the eternal joys of heaven,
Am not tormented with ten thousand hells,
In being depriv'd of everlasting bliss?
O, Faustus, leave these frivolous demands,
Which strike a terror to my fainting soul!
FAUSTUS. What, is great Mephistophilis so passionate
For being deprived of the joys of heaven?
Learn thou of Faustus manly fortitude,
And scorn those joys thou never shalt possess.
Go bear these58 tidings to great Lucifer:
Seeing Faustus hath incurr'd eternal death
By desperate thoughts against Jove's59 deity,
Say, he surrenders up to him his soul,
So he will spare him four and twenty60 years,
Letting him live in all voluptuousness;
Having thee ever to attend on me,
To give me whatsoever I shall ask,
To tell me whatsoever I demand,
To slay mine enemies, and aid my friends,
And always be obedient to my will.
Go and return to mighty Lucifer,
And meet me in my study at midnight,
And then resolve61 me of thy master's mind.
MEPHIST. I will, Faustus.
    it.

FAUSTUS. Had I as many souls as there be stars,
I'd give them all for Mephistophilis.
By him I'll be great emperor of the world,
And make a bridge thorough62 the moving air,
To pass the ocean with a band of men;
I'll join the hills that bind the Afric shore,
And make that country63 continent to Spain,
And both contributory to my crown:
The Emperor shall not live but by my leave,
Nor any potentate of Germany.
Now that I have obtain'd what I desir'd,64
I'll live in speculation of this art,
Till Mephistophilis return again.
    it.

Enter WAGNER65 and CLOWN.

WAGNER. Sirrah boy, come hither.

CLOWN. How, boy! swowns, boy! I hope you have seen many boys
with such pickadevaunts66 as I have: boy, quotha!

WAGNER. Tell me, sirrah, hast thou any comings in?

CLOWN. Ay, and goings out too; you may see else.

WAGNER. Alas, poor slave! see how poverty jesteth in his nakedness!
the villain is bare and out of service, and so hungry, that I know
he would give his soul to the devil for a shoulder of mutton,
though it were blood-raw.

CLOWN. How! my soul to the devil for a shoulder of mutton, though
'twere blood-raw! not so, good friend: by'r lady,67 I had need
have it well roasted, and good sauce to it, if I pay so dear.

WAGNER. Well, wilt thou serve me, and I'll make thee go like
Qui mihi discipulus?68

CLOWN. How, in verse?

WAGNER. No, sirrah; in beaten silk and staves-acre.69

CLOWN. How, how, knaves-acre! ay, I thought that was all the land
his father left him. Do you hear? I would be sorry to rob you of
your living.

WAGNER. Sirrah, I say in staves-acre.

CLOWN. Oho, oho, staves-acre! why, then, belike, if I were your
man, I should be full of vermin.70

WAGNER. So thou shalt, whether thou beest with me or no. But,
sirrah, leave your jesting, and bind yourself presently unto me
for seven years, or I'll turn all the lice about thee into
familiars,71 and they shall tear thee in pieces.

CLOWN. Do you hear, sir? you may save that labour; they are too
familiar with me already: swowns, they are as bold with my flesh
as if they had paid for their72 meat and drink.

WAGNER. Well, do you hear, sirrah? hold, take these guilders.
  Gives money.

CLOWN. Gridirons! what be they?

WAGNER. Why, French crowns.

CLOWN. Mass, but for the name of French crowns, a man were as good
have as many English counters. And what should I do with these?

WAGNER. Why, now, sirrah, thou art at an hour's warning, whensoever
or wheresoever the devil shall fetch thee.

CLOWN. No, no; here, take your gridirons again.

WAGNER. Truly, I'll none of them.

CLOWN. Truly, but you shall.

WAGNER. Bear witness I gave them him.

CLOWN. Bear witness I give them you again.

WAGNER. Well, I will cause two devils presently to fetch thee
away.–Baliol and Belcher!
CLOWN. Let your Baliol and your Belcher come here, and I'll
knock them, they were never so knocked since they were devils:
say I should kill one of them, what would folks say? "Do ye see
yonder tall fellow in the round slop?73 he has killed the devil."
So I should be called Kill-devil all the parish over.
Enter two DEVILS; and the CLOWN runs up and down crying.
WAGNER. Baliol and Belcher,–spirits, away!
    eunt DEVILS.

CLOWN. What, are they gone? a vengeance on them! they have vile74
long nails. There was a he-devil and a she-devil: I'll tell you
how you shall know them; all he-devils has horns, and all
she-devils has clifts and cloven feet.
WAGNER. Well, sirrah, follow me.
CLOWN. But, do you hear? if I should serve you, would you teach
me to raise up Banios and Belcheos?
WAGNER. I will teach thee to turn thyself to any thing, to a dog,
or a cat, or a mouse, or a rat, or any thing.
CLOWN. How! a Christian fellow to a dog, or a cat, a mouse,
or a rat! no, no, sir; if you turn me into any thing, let it be
in the likeness of a little pretty frisking flea, that I may be
here and there and every where: O, I'll tickle the pretty wenches'
plackets! I'll be amongst them, i'faith.
WAGNER. Well, sirrah, come.
CLOWN. But, do you hear, Wagner?
WAGNER. How!–Baliol and Belcher!
CLOWN. O Lord! I pray, sir, let Banio and Belcher go sleep.
WAGNER. Villain, call me Master Wagner, and let thy left eye be
diametarily fixed upon my right heel, with quasi vestigiis
nostris75 insistere.
    it.

CLOWN. God forgive me, he speaks Dutch fustian. Well, I'll follow
him; I'll serve him, that's flat.
    it.

FAUSTUS discovered in his study.
FAUSTUS. Now, Faustus, must
Thou needs be damn'd, and canst thou not be sav'd:
What boots it, then, to think of God or heaven?
Away with such vain fancies, and despair;
Despair in God, and trust in Belzebub:
Now go not backward; no, Faustus, be resolute:
Why waver'st thou? O, something soundeth in mine ears,

"Abjure this magic, turn to God again!"
Ay, and Faustus will turn to God again.
To God? he loves thee not;
The god thou serv'st is thine own appetite,
Wherein is fix'd the love of Belzebub:
To him I'll build an altar and a church,
And offer lukewarm blood of new-born babes.
Enter GOOD ANGEL and EVIL ANGEL.
GOOD ANGEL. Sweet Faustus, leave that execrable art.
FAUSTUS. Contrition, prayer, repentance–what of them?
GOOD ANGEL. O, they are means to bring thee unto heaven!
EVIL ANGEL. Rather illusions, fruits of lunacy,
That make men foolish that do trust them most.
GOOD ANGEL. Sweet Faustus, think of heaven and heavenly things.
EVIL ANGEL. No, Faustus; think of honour and of76 wealth.
    eunt ANGELS.

FAUSTUS. Of wealth!
Why, the signiory of Embden shall be mine.
When Mephistophilis shall stand by me,
What god can hurt thee, Faustus? thou art safe
Cast no more doubts.–Come, Mephistophilis,
And bring glad tidings from great Lucifer;–
Is't not midnight?–come, Mephistophilis,
Veni, veni, Mephistophile!
Enter MEPHISTOPHILIS.
Now tell me77 what says Lucifer, thy lord?
MEPHIST. That I shall wait on Faustus whilst he lives,78
So he will buy my service with his soul.
FAUSTUS. Already Faustus hath hazarded that for thee.
MEPHIST. But, Faustus, thou must bequeath it solemnly,
And write a deed of gift with thine own blood;
For that security craves great Lucifer.
If thou deny it, I will back to hell.
FAUSTUS. Stay, Mephistophilis, and tell me, what good will my soul
do thy lord?
MEPHIST. Enlarge his kingdom.
FAUSTUS. Is that the reason why79 he tempts us thus?
MEPHIST. Solamen miseris socios habuisse doloris.80
FAUSTUS. Why,81 have you any pain that torture82 others!
MEPHIST. As great as have the human souls of men.
But, tell me, Faustus, shall I have thy soul?
And I will be thy slave, and wait on thee,
And give thee more than thou hast wit to ask.
FAUSTUS. Ay, Mephistophilis, I give it thee.

MEPHIST. Then, Faustus,83 stab thine arm courageously,
And bind thy soul, that at some certain day
Great Lucifer may claim it as his own;
And then be thou as great as Lucifer.
FAUSTUS. [Stabbing his arm] Lo, Mephistophilis, for love of thee,
I cut mine arm, and with my proper blood
Assure my soul to be great Lucifer's,
Chief lord and regent of perpetual night!
View here the blood that trickles from mine arm,
And let it be propitious for my wish.
MEPHIST. But, Faustus, thou must
Write it in manner of a deed of gift.
FAUSTUS. Ay, so I will [Writes]. But, Mephistophilis,
My blood congeals, and I can write no more.
MEPHIST. I'll fetch thee fire to dissolve it straight.
    it.

FAUSTUS. What might the staying of my blood portend?
Is it unwilling I should write this bill?84
Why streams it not, that I may write afresh?
FAUSTUS GIVES TO THEE HIS SOUL: ah, there it stay'd!
Why shouldst thou not? is not thy soul shine own?
Then write again, FAUSTUS GIVES TO THEE HIS SOUL.
Re-enter MEPHISTOPHILIS with a chafer of coals.
MEPHIST. Here's fire; come, Faustus, set it on.85
FAUSTUS. So, now the blood begins to clear again;
Now will I make an end immediately.
    Writes.

MEPHIST. O, what will not I do to obtain his soul?
    Aside.

FAUSTUS. Consummatum est; this bill is ended,
And Faustus hath bequeath'd his soul to Lucifer.
But what is this inscription86 on mine arm?
Homo, fuge: whither should I fly?
If unto God, he'll throw me87 down to hell.
My senses are deceiv'd; here's nothing writ:–
I see it plain; here in this place is writ,
Homo, fuge: yet shall not Faustus fly.
MEPHIST. I'll fetch him somewhat to delight his mind.
    Aside, and then exit.

Re-enter MEPHISTOPHILIS with DEVILS, who give crowns
and rich apparel to FAUSTUS, dance, and then depart.
FAUSTUS. Speak, Mephistophilis, what means this show?
MEPHIST. Nothing, Faustus, but to delight thy mind withal,

And to shew thee what magic can perform.
FAUSTUS. But may I raise up spirits when I please?
MEPHIST. Ay, Faustus, and do greater things than these.
FAUSTUS. Then there's enough for a thousand souls.
Here, Mephistophilis, receive this scroll,
A deed of gift of body and of soul:
But yet conditionally that thou perform
All articles prescrib'd between us both.
MEPHIST. Faustus, I swear by hell and Lucifer
To effect all promises between us made!
FAUSTUS. Then hear me read them. [Reads] ON THESE CONDITIONS
FOLLOWING. FIRST, THAT FAUSTUS MAY BE A SPIRIT IN FORM AND
SUBSTANCE. SECONDLY, THAT MEPHISTOPHILIS SHALL BE HIS SERVANT,
AND AT HIS COMMAND. THIRDLY, THAT MEPHISTOPHILIS SHALL DO FOR
HIM,
AND BRING HIM WHATSOEVER HE DESIRES.88 FOURTHLY, THAT HE SHALL
BE IN HIS CHAMBER OR HOUSE INVISIBLE. LASTLY, THAT HE SHALL AP-
PEAR
TO THE SAID JOHN FAUSTUS, AT ALL TIMES, IN WHAT FORM OR SHAPE
SOEVER HE PLEASE. I, JOHN FAUSTUS, OF WERTENBERG, DOCTOR, BY
THESE PRESENTS, DO GIVE BOTH BODY AND SOUL TO LUCIFER PRINCE
OF
THE EAST, AND HIS MINISTER MEPHISTOPHILIS; AND FURTHERMORE
GRANT
UNTO THEM, THAT,89 TWENTY-FOUR YEARS BEING EXPIRED, THE ARTI-
CLES
ABOVE-WRITTEN INVIOLATE, FULL POWER TO FETCH OR CARRY THE
SAID
JOHN FAUSTUS, BODY AND SOUL, FLESH, BLOOD, OR GOODS, INTO THEIR
HABITATION WHERESOEVER. BY ME, JOHN FAUSTUS.
MEPHIST. Speak, Faustus, do you deliver this as your deed?
FAUSTUS. Ay, take it, and the devil give thee good on't!
MEPHIST. Now, Faustus, ask what thou wilt.
FAUSTUS. First will I question with thee about hell.
Tell me, where is the place that men call hell?
MEPHIST. Under the heavens.
FAUSTUS. Ay, but whereabout?
MEPHIST. Within the bowels of these90 elements,
Where we are tortur'd and remain for ever:
Hell hath no limits, nor is circumscrib'd
In one self place; for where we are is hell,
And where hell is, there91 must we ever be:
And, to conclude, when all the world dissolves,
And every creature shall be purified,
All places shall be hell that arc92 not heaven.

FAUSTUS. Come, I think hell's a fable.
MEPHIST. Ay, think so still, till experience change thy mind.
FAUSTUS. Why, think'st thou, then, that Faustus shall be damn'd?
MEPHIST. Ay, of necessity, for here's the scroll
Wherein thou hast given thy soul to Lucifer.
FAUSTUS. Ay, and body too: but what of that?
Think'st thou that Faustus is so fond93 to imagine
That, after this life, there is any pain?
Tush, these are trifles and mere old wives' tales.
MEPHIST. But, Faustus, I am an instance to prove the contrary,
For I am damn'd, and am now in hell.
FAUSTUS. How! now in hell!
Nay, an this be hell, I'll willingly be damn'd here:
What! walking, disputing, c.94
But, leaving off this, let me have a wife,95
The fairest maid in Germany;
For I am wanton and lascivious,
And cannot live without a wife.
MEPHIST. How! a wife!
I prithee, Faustus, talk not of a wife.
FAUSTUS. Nay, sweet Mephistophilis, fetch me one, for I will have
one.
MEPHIST. Well, thou wilt have one? Sit there till I come: I'll
fetch thee a wife in the devil's name.
  it.

Re-enter MEPHISTOPHILIS with a DEVIL drest like a WOMAN,
with fire-works.
MEPHIST. Tell me,96 Faustus, how dost thou like thy wife?
FAUSTUS. A plague on her for a hot whore!
MEPHIST. Tut, Faustus,
Marriage is but a ceremonial toy;
If thou lovest me, think no97 more of it.
I'll cull thee out the fairest courtezans,
And bring them every morning to thy bed:
She whom thine eye shall like, thy heart shall have,
Be she as chaste as was Penelope,
As wise as Saba,98 or as beautiful
As was bright Lucifer before his fall.
Hold, take this book, peruse it thoroughly:
  Gives book.

The iterating99 of these lines brings gold;
The framing of this circle on the ground
Brings whirlwinds, tempests, thunder, and lightning;
Pronounce this thrice devoutly to thyself,

And men in armour shall appear to thee,
Ready to execute what thou desir'st.
FAUSTUS. Thanks, Mephistophilis: yet fain would I have a book
wherein I might behold all spells and incantations, that I
might raise up spirits when I please.
MEPHIST. Here they are in this book.
    Turns to them.

FAUSTUS. Now would I have a book where I might see all characters
and planets of the heavens, that I might know their motions and
dispositions.
MEPHIST. Here they are too.
    Turns to them.

FAUSTUS. Nay, let me have one book more,–and then I have done,–
wherein I might see all plants, herbs, and trees, that grow upon
the earth.
MEPHIST. Here they be.
FAUSTUS. O, thou art deceived.
MEPHIST. Tut, I warrant thee.
    Turns to them.

FAUSTUS. When I behold the heavens, then I repent,
And curse thee, wicked Mephistophilis,
Because thou hast depriv'd me of those joys.
MEPHIST. Why, Faustus,
Thinkest thou heaven is such a glorious thing?
I tell thee, 'tis not half so fair as thou,
Or any man that breathes on earth.
FAUSTUS. How prov'st thou that?
MEPHIST. 'Twas made for man, therefore is man more excellent.
FAUSTUS. If it were made for man, 'twas made for me:
I will renounce this magic and repent.
Enter GOOD ANGEL and EVIL ANGEL.
GOOD ANGEL. Faustus, repent; yet God will pity thee.
EVIL ANGEL. Thou art a spirit; God cannot pity thee.
FAUSTUS. Who buzzeth in mine ears I am a spirit?
Be I a devil, yet God may pity me;
Ay, God will pity me, if I repent.
EVIL ANGEL. Ay, but Faustus never shall repent.
    eunt ANGELS.

FAUSTUS. My heart's so harden'd, I cannot repent:
Scarce can I name salvation, faith, or heaven,
But fearful echoes thunder in mine ears,
"Faustus, thou art damn'd!" then swords, and knives,
Poison, guns, halters, and envenom'd steel

Are laid before me to despatch myself;
And long ere this I should have slain myself,
Had not sweet pleasure conquer'd deep despair.
Have not I made blind Homer sing to me
Of Alexander's love and Oenon's death?
And hath not he, that built the walls of Thebes
With ravishing sound of his melodious harp,
Made music with my Mephistophilis?
Why should I die, then, or basely despair?
I am resolv'd; Faustus shall ne'er repent.–
Come, Mephistophilis, let us dispute again,
And argue of divine astrology.100
Tell me, are there many heavens above the moon
Are all celestial bodies but one globe,
As is the substance of this centric earth?
MEPHIST. As are the elements, such are the spheres,
Mutually folded in each other's orb,
And, Faustus,
All jointly move upon one axletree,
Whose terminine is term'd the world's wide pole;
Nor are the names of Saturn, Mars, or Jupiter
Feign'd, but are erring101 stars.
FAUSTUS. But, tell me, have they all one motion, both situ et
tempore?
MEPHIST. All jointly move from east to west in twenty-four hours
upon the poles of the world; but differ in their motion upon
the poles of the zodiac.
FAUSTUS. Tush,
These slender trifles Wagner can decide:
Hath Mephistophilis no greater skill?
Who knows not the double motion of the planets?
The first is finish'd in a natural day;
The second thus; as Saturn in thirty years; Jupiter in twelve;
Mars in four; the Sun, Venus, and Mercury in a year; the Moon in
twenty-eight days. Tush, these are freshmen's102 suppositions.
But, tell me, hath every sphere a dominion or intelligentia?
MEPHIST. Ay.
FAUSTUS. How many heavens or spheres are there?
MEPHIST. Nine; the seven planets, the firmament, and the empyreal
heaven.
FAUSTUS. Well, resolve103 me in this question; why have we not
conjunctions, oppositions, aspects, eclipses, all at one time,
but in some years we have more, in some less?
MEPHIST. Per inoequalem motum respectu totius.
FAUSTUS. Well, I am answered. Tell me who made the world?

MEPHIST. I will not.

FAUSTUS. Sweet Mephistophilis, tell me.

MEPHIST. Move me not, for I will not tell thee.

FAUSTUS. Villain, have I not bound thee to tell me any thing?

MEPHIST. Ay, that is not against our kingdom; but this is. Think thou on hell, Faustus, for thou art damned.

FAUSTUS. Think, Faustus, upon God that made the world.

MEPHIST. Remember this.
  It.

FAUSTUS. Ay, go, accursed spirit, to ugly hell!
'Tis thou hast damn'd distressed Faustus' soul.
Is't not too late?
Re-enter GOOD ANGEL and EVIL ANGEL.
EVIL ANGEL. Too late.
GOOD ANGEL. Never too late, if Faustus can repent.
EVIL ANGEL. If thou repent, devils shall tear thee in pieces.
GOOD ANGEL. Repent, and they shall never raze thy skin.
  eunt ANGELS.

FAUSTUS. Ah, Christ, my Saviour,
Seek to save104 distressed Faustus' soul!
Enter LUCIFER, BELZEBUB, and MEPHISTOPHILIS.
LUCIFER. Christ cannot save thy soul, for he is just:
There's none but I have interest in the same.
FAUSTUS. O, who art thou that look'st so terrible?
LUCIFER. I am Lucifer,
And this is my companion-prince in hell.
FAUSTUS. O, Faustus, they are come to fetch away thy soul!
LUCIFER. We come to tell thee thou dost injure us;
Thou talk'st of Christ, contrary to thy promise:
Thou shouldst not think of God: think of the devil,
And of his dam too.
FAUSTUS. Nor will I henceforth: pardon me in this,
And Faustus vows never to look to heaven,
Never to name God, or to pray to him,
To burn his Scriptures, slay his ministers,
And make my spirits pull his churches down.
LUCIFER. Do so, and we will highly gratify thee. Faustus, we are come from hell to shew thee some pastime: sit down, and thou shalt see all the Seven Deadly Sins appear in their proper shapes.
FAUSTUS. That sight will be as pleasing unto me,
As Paradise was to Adam, the first day
Of his creation.
LUCIFER. Talk not of Paradise nor creation; but mark this show: talk of the devil, and nothing else.–Come away!

Enter the SEVEN DEADLY SINS.105

Now, Faustus, examine them of their several names and dispositions.

FAUSTUS. What art thou, the first?

PRIDE. I am Pride. I disdain to have any parents. I am like to
Ovid's flea; I can creep into every corner of a wench; sometimes,
like a perriwig, I sit upon her brow; or, like a fan of feathers,
I kiss her lips; indeed, I do–what do I not? But, fie, what a
scent is here! I'll not speak another word, except the ground
were perfumed, and covered with cloth of arras.

FAUSTUS. What art thou, the second?

COVETOUSNESS. I am Covetousness, begotten of an old churl, in an
old leathern bag: and, might I have my wish, I would desire that
this house and all the people in it were turned to gold, that I
might lock you up in my good chest: O, my sweet gold!

FAUSTUS. What art thou, the third?

WRATH. I am Wrath. I had neither father nor mother: I leapt out
of a lion's mouth when I was scarce half-an-hour old; and ever
since I have run up and down the world with this case106
of rapiers, wounding myself when I had nobody to fight withal.
I was born in hell; and look to it, for some of you shall be
my father.

FAUSTUS. What art thou, the fourth?

ENVY. I am Envy, begotten of a chimney-sweeper and an oyster-wife.
I cannot read, and therefore wish all books were burnt. I am lean
with seeing others eat. O, that there would come a famine through
all the world, that all might die, and I live alone! then thou
shouldst see how fat I would be. But must thou sit, and I stand?
come down, with a vengeance!

FAUSTUS. Away, envious rascal!–What art thou, the fifth?

GLUTTONY. Who I, sir? I am Gluttony. My parents are all dead,
and the devil a penny they have left me, but a bare pension, and
that is thirty meals a-day and ten bevers,107–a small trifle
to suffice nature. O, I come of a royal parentage! my grandfather
was a Gammon of Bacon, my grandmother a Hogshead of Claret-wine;
my godfathers were these, Peter Pickle-herring and Martin
Martlemas-beef; O, but my godmother, she was a jolly gentlewoman,
and well-beloved in every good town and city; her name was Mistress
Margery March-beer. Now, Faustus, thou hast heard all my progeny;
wilt thou bid me to supper?

FAUSTUS. No, I'll see thee hanged: thou wilt eat up all my victuals.

GLUTTONY. Then the devil choke thee!

FAUSTUS. Choke thyself, glutton!–What art thou, the sixth?

SLOTH. I am Sloth. I was begotten on a sunny bank, where I have
lain ever since; and you have done me great injury to bring me
from thence: let me be carried thither again by Gluttony and

Lechery. I'll not speak another word for a king's ransom.
FAUSTUS. What are you, Mistress Minx, the seventh and last?
LECHERY. Who I, sir? I am one that loves an inch of raw mutton
better than an ell of fried stock-fish; and the first letter
of my name begins with L.108
FAUSTUS. Away, to hell, to hell!109
   eunt the SINS.

LUCIFER. Now, Faustus, how dost thou like this?
FAUSTUS. O, this feeds my soul!
LUCIFER. Tut, Faustus, in hell is all manner of delight.
FAUSTUS. O, might I see hell, and return again,
How happy were I then!
LUCIFER. Thou shalt; I will send for thee at midnight.110
In meantime take this book; peruse it throughly,
And thou shalt turn thyself into what shape thou wilt.
FAUSTUS. Great thanks, mighty Lucifer!
This will I keep as chary as my life.
LUCIFER. Farewell, Faustus, and think on the devil.
FAUSTUS. Farewell, great Lucifer.
   eunt LUCIFER and BELZEBUB.

Come, Mephistophilis.
   eunt.

Enter CHORUS.111
CHORUS. Learned Faustus,
To know the secrets of astronomy112
Graven in the book of Jove's high firmament,
Did mount himself to scale Olympus' top,
Being seated in a chariot burning bright,
Drawn by the strength of yoky dragons' necks.
He now is gone to prove cosmography,
And, as I guess, will first arrive at Rome,
To see the Pope and manner of his court,
And take some part of holy Peter's feast,
That to this day is highly solemniz'd.
   it.

Enter FAUSTUS and MEPHISTOPHILIS.113
FAUSTUS. Having now, my good Mephistophilis,
Pass'd with delight the stately town of Trier,114
Environ'd round with airy mountain-tops,
With walls of flint, and deep-entrenched lakes,
Not to be won by any conquering prince;
From Paris next,115 coasting the realm of France,
We saw the river Maine fall into Rhine,

Whose banks are set with groves of fruitful vines;
Then up to Naples, rich Campania,
Whose buildings fair and gorgeous to the eye,
The streets straight forth, and pav'd with finest brick,
Quarter the town in four equivalents:
There saw we learned Maro's golden tomb,
The way he cut,116 an English mile in length,
Thorough a rock of stone, in one night's space;
From thence to Venice, Padua, and the rest,
In one of which a sumptuous temple stands,117
That threats the stars with her aspiring top.
Thus hitherto hath Faustus spent his time:
But tell me now what resting-place is this?
Hast thou, as erst I did command,
Conducted me within the walls of Rome?
MEPHIST. Faustus, I have; and, because we will not be unprovided,
I have taken up his Holiness' privy-chamber for our use.
FAUSTUS. I hope his Holiness will bid us welcome.
MEPHIST.
Tut, 'tis no matter; man; we'll be bold with his good cheer.
And now, my Faustus, that thou mayst perceive
What Rome containeth to delight thee with,
Know that this city stands upon seven hills
That underprop the groundwork of the same:
Just through the midst118 runs flowing Tiber's stream
With winding banks that cut it in two parts;
Over the which four stately bridges lean,
That make safe passage to each part of Rome:
Upon the bridge call'd Ponte119 Angelo
Erected is a castle passing strong,
Within whose walls such store of ordnance are,
And double cannons fram'd of carved brass,
As match the days within one complete year;
Besides the gates, and high pyramides,
Which Julius Caesar brought from Africa.
FAUSTUS. Now, by the kingdoms of infernal rule,
Of Styx, of120 Acheron, and the fiery lake
Of ever-burning Phlegethon, I swear
That I do long to see the monuments
And situation of bright-splendent Rome:
Come, therefore, let's away.
MEPHIST. Nay, Faustus, stay: I know you'd fain see the Pope,
And take some part of holy Peter's feast,
Where thou shalt see a troop of bald-pate friars,
Whose summum bonum is in belly-cheer.

FAUSTUS. Well, I'm content to compass then some sport,
And by their folly make us merriment.
Then charm me, that I121
May be invisible, to do what I please,
Unseen of any whilst I stay in Rome.
    Mephistophilis charms him.

MEPHIST. So, Faustus; now
Do what thou wilt, thou shalt not be discern'd.
Sound a Sonnet.122 Enter the POPE and the CARDINAL OF
LORRAIN to the banquet, with FRIARS attending.
POPE. My Lord of Lorrain, will't please you draw near?
FAUSTUS. Fall to, and the devil choke you, an you spare!
POPE. How now! who's that which spake?–Friars, look about.
FIRST FRIAR. Here's nobody, if it like your Holiness.
POPE. My lord, here is a dainty dish was sent me from the Bishop
of Milan.
FAUSTUS. I thank you, sir.
    Snatches the dish.

POPE. How now! who's that which snatched the meat from me? will
no man look?–My lord, this dish was sent me from the Cardinal
of Florence.
FAUSTUS. You say true; I'll ha't.
    Snatches the dish.

POPE. What, again!–My lord, I'll drink to your grace.
FAUSTUS. I'll pledge your grace.
    Snatches the cup.

C. OF LOR. My lord, it may be some ghost, newly crept out of
Purgatory, come to beg a pardon of your Holiness.
POPE. It may be so.–Friars, prepare a dirge to lay the fury
of this ghost.–Once again, my lord, fall to.
    The POPE crosses himself.

FAUSTUS. What, are you crossing of yourself?
Well, use that trick no more, I would advise you.
    The POPE crosses himself again.

Well, there's the second time. Aware the third;
I give you fair warning.
    The POPE crosses himself again, and FAUSTUS hits him a box
of the ear; and they all run away.

Come on, Mephistophilis; what shall we do?
MEPHIST. Nay, I know not: we shall be cursed with bell, book,

and candle.

FAUSTUS. How! bell, book, and candle,–candle, book, and bell,–
Forward and backward, to curse Faustus to hell!
Anon you shall hear a hog grunt, a calf bleat, and an ass bray,
Because it is Saint Peter's holiday.
Re-enter all the FRIARS to sing the Dirge.
FIRST FRIAR.
Come, brethren, let's about our business with good devotion.
They sing.
CURSED BE HE THAT STOLE AWAY HIS HOLINESS' MEAT FROM THE
TABLE! maledicat Dominus!
CURSED BE HE THAT STRUCK HIS HOLINESS A BLOW ON THE FACE!
maledicat Dominus!
CURSED BE HE THAT TOOK FRIAR SANDELO A BLOW ON THE PATE!
maledicat Dominus!
CURSED BE HE THAT DISTURBETH OUR HOLY DIRGE! maledicat
Dominus!
CURSED BE HE THAT TOOK AWAY HIS HOLINESS' WINE! maledicat
Dominus? ['?' sic]
Et omnes Sancti! Amen!
   MEPHISTOPHILIS and FAUSTUS beat the FRIARS, and fling
fire-works among them; and so exeunt.

Enter CHORUS.
CHORUS. When Faustus had with pleasure ta'en the view
Of rarest things, and royal courts of kings,
He stay'd his course, and so returned home;
Where such as bear his absence but with grief,
I mean his friends and near'st companions,
Did gratulate his safety with kind words,
And in their conference of what befell,
Touching his journey through the world and air,
They put forth questions of astrology,
Which Faustus answer'd with such learned skill
As they admir'd and wonder'd at his wit.
Now is his fame spread forth in every land:
Amongst the rest the Emperor is one,
Carolus the Fifth, at whose palace now
Faustus is feasted 'mongst his noblemen.
What there he did, in trial of his art,
I leave untold; your eyes shall see['t] perform'd.
   it.

Enter ROBIN123 the Ostler, with a book in his hand.
ROBIN. O, this is admirable! here I ha' stolen one of Doctor
Faustus' conjuring-books, and, i'faith, I mean to search some

circles for my own use. Now will I make all the maidens in our
parish dance at my pleasure, stark naked, before me; and so
by that means I shall see more than e'er I felt or saw yet.

Enter RALPH, calling ROBIN.

RALPH. Robin, prithee, come away; there's a gentleman tarries
to have his horse, and he would have his things rubbed and made
clean: he keeps such a chafing with my mistress about it; and
she has sent me to look thee out; prithee, come away.

ROBIN. Keep out, keep out, or else you are blown up, you are
dismembered, Ralph: keep out, for I am about a roaring piece
of work.

RALPH. Come, what doest thou with that same book? thou canst
not read?

ROBIN. Yes, my master and mistress shall find that I can read,
he for his forehead, she for her private study; she's born to
bear with me, or else my art fails.

RALPH. Why, Robin, what book is that?

ROBIN. What book! why, the most intolerable book for conjuring
that e'er was invented by any brimstone devil.

RALPH. Canst thou conjure with it?

ROBIN. I can do all these things easily with it; first, I can
make thee drunk with ippocras124 at any tabern125 in Europe
for nothing; that's one of my conjuring works.

RALPH. Our Master Parson says that's nothing.

ROBIN. True, Ralph: and more, Ralph, if thou hast any mind to
Nan Spit, our kitchen-maid, then turn her and wind her to thy own
use, as often as thou wilt, and at midnight.

RALPH. O, brave, Robin! shall I have Nan Spit, and to mine own
use? On that condition I'll feed thy devil with horse-bread as
long as he lives, of free cost.

ROBIN. No more, sweet Ralph: let's go and make clean our boots,
which lie foul upon our hands, and then to our conjuring in the
devil's name.
      eunt.

Enter ROBIN and RALPH126 with a silver goblet.

ROBIN. Come, Ralph: did not I tell thee, we were for ever made
by this Doctor Faustus' book? ecce, signum! here's a simple
purchase127 for horse-keepers: our horses shall eat no hay as
long as this lasts.

RALPH. But, Robin, here comes the Vintner.

ROBIN. Hush! I'll gull him supernaturally.

Enter VINTNER.

Drawer,128 I hope all is paid; God be with you!–Come, Ralph.

VINTNER. Soft, sir; a word with you. I must yet have a goblet paid from you, ere you go.

ROBIN. I a goblet, Ralph, I a goblet!–I scorn you; and you are
but a, c. I a goblet! search me.

VINTNER. I mean so, sir, with your favour.
    Searches ROBIN.

ROBIN. How say you now?

VINTNER. I must say somewhat to your fellow.–You, sir!

RALPH. Me, sir! me, sir! search your fill. [VINTNER searches him.]
Now, sir, you may be ashamed to burden honest men with a matter
of truth.

VINTNER. Well, tone129 of you hath this goblet about you.

ROBIN. You lie, drawer, 'tis afore me [Aside].–Sirrah you, I'll
teach you to impeach honest men;–stand by;–I'll scour you for
a goblet;–stand aside you had best, I charge you in the name of
Belzebub.–Look to the goblet, Ralph [Aside to RALPH].

VINTNER. What mean you, sirrah?

ROBIN. I'll tell you what I mean. [Reads from a book] Sanctobulorum
Periphrasticon–nay, I'll tickle you, Vintner.–Look to the goblet,
Ralph [Aside to RALPH].–[Reads] Polypragmos Belseborams framanto
pacostiphos tostu, Mephistophilis, c.

Enter MEPHISTOPHILIS, sets squibs at their backs, and then
exit. They run about.

VINTNER. O, nomine Domini! what meanest thou, Robin? thou hast no
goblet.

RALPH. Peccatum peccatorum!–Here's thy goblet, good Vintner.
    Gives the goblet to VINTNER, who exit.

ROBIN. Misericordia pro nobis! what shall I do? Good devil, forgive
me now, and I'll never rob thy library more.

Re-enter MEPHISTOPHILIS.

MEPHIST. Monarch of Hell,130 under whose black survey
Great potentates do kneel with awful fear,
Upon whose altars thousand souls do lie,
How am I vexed with these villains' charms?
From Constantinople am I hither come,
Only for pleasure of these damned slaves.

ROBIN. How, from Constantinople! you have had a great journey:
will you take sixpence in your purse to pay for your supper, and
be gone?

MEPHIST. Well, villains, for your presumption, I transform thee
into an ape, and thee into a dog; and so be gone!
    it.

ROBIN. How, into an ape! that's brave: I'll have fine sport with
the boys; I'll get nuts and apples enow.

RALPH. And I must be a dog.
ROBIN. I'faith, thy head will never be out of the pottage-pot.
   eunt.

Enter EMPEROR,131 FAUSTUS, and a KNIGHT, with ATTENDANTS.
EMPEROR. Master Doctor Faustus,132 I have heard strange report
of thy knowledge in the black art, how that none in my empire
nor in the whole world can compare with thee for the rare effects
of magic: they say thou hast a familiar spirit, by whom thou canst
accomplish what thou list. This, therefore, is my request, that
thou let me see some proof of thy skill, that mine eyes may be
witnesses to confirm what mine ears have heard reported: and here
I swear to thee, by the honour of mine imperial crown, that,
whatever thou doest, thou shalt be no ways prejudiced or endamaged.
KNIGHT. I'faith, he looks much like a conjurer.
   Aside.

FAUSTUS. My gracious sovereign, though I must confess myself far
inferior to the report men have published, and nothing answerable
to the honour of your imperial majesty, yet, for that love and duty
binds me thereunto, I am content to do whatsoever your majesty
shall command me.
EMPEROR. Then, Doctor Faustus, mark what I shall say.
As I was sometime solitary set
Within my closet, sundry thoughts arose
About the honour of mine ancestors,
How they had won133 by prowess such exploits,
Got such riches, subdu'd so many kingdoms,
As we that do succeed,134 or they that shall
Hereafter possess our throne, shall
(I fear me) ne'er attain to that degree
Of high renown and great authority:
Amongst which kings is Alexander the Great,
Chief spectacle of the world's pre-eminence,
The bright135 shining of whose glorious acts
Lightens the world with his reflecting beams,
As when I hear but motion made of him,
It grieves my soul I never saw the man:
If, therefore, thou, by cunning of thine art,
Canst raise this man from hollow vaults below,
Where lies entomb'd this famous conqueror,
And bring with him his beauteous paramour,
Both in their right shapes, gesture, and attire
They us'd to wear during their time of life,
Thou shalt both satisfy my just desire,
And give me cause to praise thee whilst I live.

FAUSTUS. My gracious lord, I am ready to accomplish your request,
so far forth as by art and power of my spirit I am able to perform.
KNIGHT. I'faith, that's just nothing at all.
   Aside.

FAUSTUS. But, if it like your grace, it is not in my ability 136
to present before your eyes the true substantial bodies of those
two deceased princes, which long since are consumed to dust.
KNIGHT. Ay, marry, Master Doctor, now there's a sign of grace in
you, when you will confess the truth.
   Aside.

FAUSTUS. But such spirits as can lively resemble Alexander and
his paramour shall appear before your grace, in that manner that
they both 137 lived in, in their most flourishing estate; which
I doubt not shall sufficiently content your imperial majesty.
EMPEROR. Go to, Master Doctor; let me see them presently.
KNIGHT. Do you hear, Master Doctor? you bring Alexander and his
paramour before the Emperor!
FAUSTUS. How then, sir?
KNIGHT. I'faith, that's as true as Diana turned me to a stag.
FAUSTUS. No, sir; but, when Actaeon died, he left the horns for
you.–Mephistophilis, be gone.
   it MEPHISTOPHILIS.

KNIGHT. Nay, an you go to conjuring, I'll be gone.
   it.

FAUSTUS. I'll meet with you anon for interrupting me so.
–Here they are, my gracious lord.
Re-enter MEPHISTOPHILIS with SPIRITS in the shapes of ALEXANDER
and his PARAMOUR.
EMPEROR. Master Doctor, I heard this lady, while she lived, had a
wart or mole in her neck: how shall I know whether it be so or no?
FAUSTUS. Your highness may boldly go and see.
EMPEROR. Sure, these are no spirits, but the true substantial
bodies of those two deceased princes.
   eunt Spirits.

FAUSTUS. Wilt please your highness now to send for the knight
that was so pleasant with me here of late?
EMPEROR. One of you call him forth.
   it ATTENDANT.

Re-enter the KNIGHT with a pair of horns on his head.
How now, sir knight! why, I had thought thou hadst been a bachelor,
but now I see thou hast a wife, that not only gives thee horns,

but makes thee wear them. Feel on thy head.

KNIGHT. Thou damned wretch and execrable dog,

Bred in the concave of some monstrous rock,

How dar'st thou thus abuse a gentleman?

Villain, I say, undo what thou hast done!

FAUSTUS. O, not so fast, sir! there's no haste: but, good, are

you remembered how you crossed me in my conference with the

Emperor? I think I have met with you for it.

EMPEROR. Good Master Doctor, at my entreaty release him: he hath

done penance sufficient.

FAUSTUS. My gracious lord, not so much for the injury he offered

me here in your presence, as to delight you with some mirth, hath

Faustus worthily requited this injurious knight; which being all

I desire, I am content to release him of his horns:–and,

sir knight, hereafter speak well of scholars.–Mephistophilis,

transform him straight.138 [MEPHISTOPHILIS removes the horns.]

–Now, my good lord, having done my duty, I humbly take my leave.

EMPEROR. Farewell, Master Doctor: yet, ere you go,

Expect from me a bounteous reward.

    eunt EMPEROR, KNIGHT, and ATTENDANTS.

FAUSTUS. Now, Mephistophilis,139 the restless course

That time doth run with calm and silent foot,

Shortening my days and thread of vital life,

Calls for the payment of my latest years:

Therefore, sweet Mephistophilis, let us

Make haste to Wertenberg.

MEPHIST. What, will you go on horse-back or on foot[?]

FAUSTUS. Nay, till I'm past this fair and pleasant green,

I'll walk on foot.

Enter a HORSE-COURSER.140

HORSE-COURSER. I have been all this day seeking one Master Fustian:

mass, see where he is!–God save you, Master Doctor!

FAUSTUS. What, horse-courser! you are well met.

HORSE-COURSER. Do you hear, sir? I have brought you forty dollars

for your horse.

FAUSTUS. I cannot sell him so: if thou likest him for fifty, take

him.

HORSE-COURSER. Alas, sir, I have no more!–I pray you, speak for

me.

MEPHIST. I pray you, let him have him: he is an honest fellow,

and he has a great charge, neither wife nor child.

FAUSTUS. Well, come, give me your money [HORSE-COURSER gives

FAUSTUS the money]: my boy will deliver him to you. But I must

tell you one thing before you have him; ride him not into the water, at any hand.

HORSE-COURSER. Why, sir, will he not drink of all waters?

FAUSTUS. O, yes, he will drink of all waters; but ride him not
into the water: ride him over hedge or ditch, or where thou wilt,
but not into the water.

HORSE-COURSER. Well, sir.–Now am I made man for ever: I'll not
leave my horse for forty:141 if he had but the quality of
hey-ding-ding, hey-ding-ding, I'd make a brave living on him:
he has a buttock as slick as an eel [Aside].–Well, God b'wi'ye,
sir: your boy will deliver him me: but, hark you, sir; if my horse
be sick or ill at ease, if I bring his water to you, you'll tell
me what it is?

FAUSTUS. Away, you villain! what, dost think I am a horse-doctor?
   it HORSE-COURSER.

What art thou, Faustus, but a man condemn'd to die?
Thy fatal time doth draw to final end;
Despair doth drive distrust into142 my thoughts:
Confound these passions with a quiet sleep:
Tush, Christ did call the thief upon the Cross;
Then rest thee, Faustus, quiet in conceit.
   Sleeps in his chair.

Re-enter HORSE-COURSER, all wet, crying.

HORSE-COURSER. Alas, alas! Doctor Fustian, quoth a? mass, Doctor
Lopus143 was never such a doctor: has given me a purgation, has
purged me of forty dollars; I shall never see them more. But yet,
like an ass as I was, I would not be ruled by him, for he bade me
I should ride him into no water: now I, thinking my horse had had
some rare quality that he would not have had me know of,144 I,
like a venturous youth, rid him into the deep pond at the town's
end. I was no sooner in the middle of the pond, but my horse
vanished away, and I sat upon a bottle of hay, never so near
drowning in my life. But I'll seek out my doctor, and have my
forty dollars again, or I'll make it the dearest horse!–O,
yonder is his snipper-snapper.–Do you hear? you, hey-pass,145
where's your master?

MEPHIST. Why, sir, what would you? you cannot speak with him.

HORSE-COURSER. But I will speak with him.

MEPHIST. Why, he's fast asleep: come some other time.

HORSE-COURSER. I'll speak with him now, or I'll break his
glass-windows about his ears.

MEPHIST. I tell thee, he has not slept this eight nights.

HORSE-COURSER. An he have not slept this eight weeks, I'll
speak with him.

MEPHIST. See, where he is, fast asleep.

HORSE-COURSER. Ay, this is he.–God save you, Master Doctor,
Master Doctor, Master Doctor Fustian! forty dollars, forty dollars
for a bottle of hay!
MEPHIST. Why, thou seest he hears thee not.
HORSE-COURSER. So-ho, ho! so-ho, ho! [Hollows in his ear.] No,
will you not wake? I'll make you wake ere I go. [Pulls FAUSTUS
by the leg, and pulls it away.] Alas, I am undone! what shall
I do?
FAUSTUS. O, my leg, my leg!–Help, Mephistophilis! call the
officers.–My leg, my leg!
MEPHIST. Come, villain, to the constable.
HORSE-COURSER. O Lord, sir, let me go, and I'll give you forty
dollars more!
MEPHIST. Where be they?
HORSE-COURSER. I have none about me: come to my ostry,146
and I'll give them you.
MEPHIST. Be gone quickly.
    HORSE-COURSER runs away.

FAUSTUS. What, is he gone? farewell he! Faustus has his leg again,
and the Horse-courser, I take it, a bottle of hay for his labour:
well, this trick shall cost him forty dollars more.
Enter WAGNER.
How now, Wagner! what's the news with thee?
WAGNER. Sir, the Duke of Vanholt doth earnestly entreat your
company.
FAUSTUS. The Duke of Vanholt! an honourable gentleman, to whom
I must be no niggard of my cunning.147–Come, Mephistophilis,
let's away to him.
    eunt.

Enter the DUKE OF VANHOLT, the DUCHESS, and FAUSTUS.148
DUKE. Believe me, Master Doctor, this merriment hath much pleased
me.
FAUSTUS. My gracious lord, I am glad it contents you so well.
–But it may be, madam, you take no delight in this. I have heard
that great-bellied women do long for some dainties or other: what
is it, madam? tell me, and you shall have it.
DUCHESS. Thanks, good Master Doctor: and, for I see your courteous
intent to pleasure me, I will not hide from you the thing my heart
desires; and, were it now summer, as it is January and the dead
time of the winter, I would desire no better meat than a dish
of ripe grapes.
FAUSTUS. Alas, madam, that's nothing!–Mephistophilis, be gone.
    it MEPHISTOPHILIS.
Were it a greater thing than this, so it

would content you, you should have it.
Re-enter MEPHISTOPHILIS with grapes.
Here they be, madam: wilt please you taste on them?
DUKE. Believe me, Master Doctor, this makes me wonder above the
rest, that being in the dead time of winter and in the month of
January, how you should come by these grapes.
FAUSTUS. If it like your grace, the year is divided into two
circles over the whole world, that, when it is here winter with
us, in the contrary circle it is summer with them, as in India,
Saba,149 and farther countries in the east; and by means of a
swift spirit that I have, I had them brought hither, as you see.
–How do you like them, madam? be they good?
DUCHESS. Believe me, Master Doctor, they be the best grapes that
e'er I tasted in my life before.
FAUSTUS. I am glad they content you so, madam.
DUKE. Come, madam, let us in, where you must well reward this
learned man for the great kindness he hath shewed to you.
DUCHESS. And so I will, my lord; and, whilst I live, rest
beholding150 for this courtesy.
FAUSTUS. I humbly thank your grace.
DUKE. Come, Master Doctor, follow us, and receive your reward.
    eunt.

Enter WAGNER.151
WAGNER. I think my master means to die shortly,
For he hath given to me all his goods:152
And yet, methinks, if that death were near,
He would not banquet, and carouse, and swill
Amongst the students, as even now he doth,
Who are at supper with such belly-cheer
As Wagner ne'er beheld in all his life.
See, where they come! belike the feast is ended.
    it.

Enter FAUSTUS with two or three SCHOLARS, and MEPHISTOPHILIS.
FIRST SCHOLAR. Master Doctor Faustus, since our conference about
fair ladies, which was the beautifulest in all the world, we have
determined with ourselves that Helen of Greece was the admirablest
lady that ever lived: therefore, Master Doctor, if you will do us
that favour, as to let us see that peerless dame of Greece, whom
all the world admires for majesty, we should think ourselves much
beholding unto you.
FAUSTUS. Gentlemen,
For that I know your friendship is unfeign'd,
And Faustus' custom is not to deny
The just requests of those that wish him well,

You shall behold that peerless dame of Greece,
No otherways for pomp and majesty
Than when Sir Paris cross'd the seas with her,
And brought the spoils to rich Dardania.
Be silent, then, for danger is in words.
    Music sounds, and HELEN passeth over the stage.
153
SECOND SCHOLAR. Too simple is my wit to tell her praise,
Whom all the world admires for majesty.
THIRD SCHOLAR. No marvel though the angry Greeks pursu'd
With ten years' war the rape of such a queen,
Whose heavenly beauty passeth all compare.
FIRST SCHOLAR. Since we have seen the pride of Nature's works,
And only paragon of excellence,
Let us depart; and for this glorious deed
Happy and blest be Faustus evermore!
FAUSTUS. Gentlemen, farewell: the same I wish to you.
    eunt SCHOLARS.

Enter an OLD MAN.154
OLD MAN. Ah, Doctor Faustus, that I might prevail
To guide thy steps unto the way of life,
By which sweet path thou mayst attain the goal
That shall conduct thee to celestial rest!
Break heart, drop blood, and mingle it with tears,
Tears falling from repentant heaviness
Of thy most vile155 and loathsome filthiness,
The stench whereof corrupts the inward soul
With such flagitious crimes of heinous sin156
As no commiseration may expel,
But mercy, Faustus, of thy Saviour sweet,
Whose blood alone must wash away thy guilt.
FAUSTUS. Where art thou, Faustus? wretch, what hast thou done?
Damn'd art thou, Faustus, damn'd; despair and die!
Hell calls for right, and with a roaring voice
Says, "Faustus, come; thine hour is almost157 come;"
And Faustus now158 will come to do thee right.
    MEPHISTOPHILIS gives him a dagger.

OLD MAN. Ah, stay, good Faustus, stay thy desperate steps!
I see an angel hovers o'er thy head,
And, with a vial full of precious grace,
Offers to pour the same into thy soul:
Then call for mercy, and avoid despair.
FAUSTUS. Ah, my sweet friend, I feel
Thy words to comfort my distressed soul!

Leave me a while to ponder on my sins.
OLD MAN. I go, sweet Faustus; but with heavy cheer,
Fearing the ruin of thy hopeless soul.
    it.

FAUSTUS. Accursed Faustus, where is mercy now?
I do repent; and yet I do despair:
Hell strives with grace for conquest in my breast:
What shall I do to shun the snares of death?
MEPHIST. Thou traitor, Faustus, I arrest thy soul
For disobedience to my sovereign lord:
Revolt, or I'll in piece-meal tear thy flesh.
FAUSTUS. Sweet Mephistophilis, entreat thy lord
To pardon my unjust presumption,
And with my blood again I will confirm
My former vow I made to Lucifer.
MEPHIST. Do it, then, quickly,159 with unfeigned heart,
Lest greater danger do attend thy drift.
FAUSTUS. Torment, sweet friend, that base and crooked age,
That durst dissuade me from thy Lucifer,
With greatest torments that our hell affords.
MEPHIST. His faith is great; I cannot touch his soul;
But what I may afflict his body with
I will attempt, which is but little worth.
FAUSTUS. One thing, good servant,160 let me crave of thee,
To glut the longing of my heart's desire,–
That I might have unto my paramour
That heavenly Helen which I saw of late,
Whose sweet embracings may extinguish clean
Those161 thoughts that do dissuade me from my vow,
And keep mine oath I made to Lucifer.
MEPHIST. Faustus, this,162 or what else thou shalt desire,
Shall be perform'd in twinkling of an eye.
Re-enter HELEN.
FAUSTUS. Was this the face that launch'd a thousand ships,
And burnt the topless163 towers of Ilium–
Sweet Helen, make me immortal with a kiss.–
    Kisses her.

Her lips suck forth my soul: see, where it flies!–
Come, Helen, come, give me my soul again.
Here will I dwell, for heaven is164 in these lips,
And all is dross that is not Helena.
I will be Paris, and for love of thee,
Instead of Troy, shall Wertenberg be sack'd;
And I will combat with weak Menelaus,

And wear thy colours on my plumed crest;
Yea, I will wound Achilles in the heel,
And then return to Helen for a kiss.
O, thou art fairer than the evening air
Clad in the beauty of a thousand stars;
Brighter art thou than flaming Jupiter
When he appear'd to hapless Semele;
More lovely than the monarch of the sky
In wanton Arethusa's azur'd arms;
And none but thou shalt165 be my paramour!
    eunt.

Enter the OLD MAN.166
OLD MAN. Accursed Faustus, miserable man,
That from thy soul exclud'st the grace of heaven,
And fly'st the throne of his tribunal-seat!
Enter DEVILS.
Satan begins to sift me with his pride:
As in this furnace God shall try my faith,
My faith, vile hell, shall triumph over thee.
Ambitious fiends, see how the heavens smile
At your repulse, and laugh your state to scorn!
Hence, hell! for hence I fly unto my God.
    eunt,–on one side, DEVILS, on the other, OLD MAN.

Enter FAUSTUS,167 with SCHOLARS.
FAUSTUS. Ah, gentlemen!
FIRST SCHOLAR. What ails Faustus?
FAUSTUS. Ah, my sweet chamber-fellow, had I lived with thee,
then had I lived still! but now I die eternally. Look, comes
he not? comes he not?
SECOND SCHOLAR. What means Faustus?
THIRD SCHOLAR. Belike he is grown into some sickness by being
over-solitary.
FIRST SCHOLAR. If it be so, we'll have physicians to cure him.
–'Tis but a surfeit; never fear, man.
FAUSTUS. A surfeit of deadly sin, that hath damned both body
and soul.
SECOND SCHOLAR. Yet, Faustus, look up to heaven; remember God's
mercies are infinite.
FAUSTUS. But Faustus' offence can ne'er be pardoned: the serpent
that tempted Eve may be saved, but not Faustus. Ah, gentlemen,
hear me with patience, and tremble not at my speeches! Though
my heart pants and quivers to remember that I have been a student
here these thirty years, O, would I had never seen Wertenberg,
never read book! and what wonders I have done, all Germany can

witness, yea, all the world; for which Faustus hath lost both
Germany and the world, yea, heaven itself, heaven, the seat of
God, the throne of the blessed, the kingdom of joy; and must
remain in hell for ever, hell, ah, hell, for ever! Sweet friends,
what shall become of Faustus, being in hell for ever?

THIRD SCHOLAR. Yet, Faustus, call on God.

FAUSTUS. On God, whom Faustus hath abjured! on God, whom Faustus
hath blasphemed! Ah, my God, I would weep! but the devil draws in
my tears. Gush forth blood, instead of tears! yea, life and soul!
O, he stays my tongue! I would lift up my hands; but see, they
hold them, they hold them!

ALL. Who, Faustus?

FAUSTUS. Lucifer and Mephistophilis. Ah, gentlemen, I gave them
my soul for my cunning!168

ALL. God forbid!

FAUSTUS. God forbade it, indeed; but Faustus hath done it: for
vain pleasure of twenty-four years hath Faustus lost eternal joy
and felicity. I writ them a bill with mine own blood: the date
is expired; the time will come, and he will fetch me.

FIRST SCHOLAR. Why did not Faustus tell us of this before,169
that divines might have prayed for thee?

FAUSTUS. Oft have I thought to have done so; but the devil
threatened to tear me in pieces, if I named God, to fetch both
body and soul, if I once gave ear to divinity: and now 'tis too
late. Gentlemen, away, lest you perish with me.

SECOND SCHOLAR. O, what shall we do to save170 Faustus?

FAUSTUS. Talk not of me, but save yourselves, and depart.

THIRD SCHOLAR. God will strengthen me; I will stay with Faustus.

FIRST SCHOLAR. Tempt not God, sweet friend; but let us into the
next room, and there pray for him.

FAUSTUS. Ay, pray for me, pray for me; and what noise soever
ye hear,171 come not unto me, for nothing can rescue me.

SECOND SCHOLAR. Pray thou, and we will pray that God may have
mercy upon thee.

FAUSTUS. Gentlemen, farewell: if I live till morning, I'll visit
you; if not, Faustus is gone to hell.

ALL. Faustus, farewell.

   eunt SCHOLARS.–The clock strikes eleven.

FAUSTUS. Ah, Faustus,
Now hast thou but one bare hour to live,
And then thou must be damn'd perpetually!
Stand still, you ever-moving spheres of heaven,
That time may cease, and midnight never come;
Fair Nature's eye, rise, rise again, and make

Perpetual day; or let this hour be but
A year, a month, a week, a natural day,
That Faustus may repent and save his soul!
O lente,172 lente currite, noctis equi!
The stars move still, time runs, the clock will strike,
The devil will come, and Faustus must be damn'd.
O, I'll leap up to my God!–Who pulls me down?–
See, see, where Christ's blood streams in the firmament!
One drop would save my soul, half a drop: ah, my Christ!–
Ah, rend not my heart for naming of my Christ!
Yet will I call on him: O, spare me, Lucifer!–
Where is it now? 'tis gone: and see, where God
Stretcheth out his arm, and bends his ireful brows!
Mountains and hills, come, come, and fall on me,
And hide me from the heavy wrath of God!
No, no!
Then will I headlong run into the earth:
Earth, gape! O, no, it will not harbour me!
You stars that reign'd at my nativity,
Whose influence hath allotted death and hell,
Now draw up Faustus, like a foggy mist.
Into the entrails of yon labouring cloud[s],
That, when you173 vomit forth into the air,
My limbs may issue from your smoky mouths,
So that my soul may but ascend to heaven!
        The clock strikes the half-hour.

Ah, half the hour is past! 'twill all be past anon
O God,
If thou wilt not have mercy on my soul,
Yet for Christ's sake, whose blood hath ransom'd me,
Impose some end to my incessant pain;
Let Faustus live in hell a thousand years,
A hundred thousand, and at last be sav'd!
O, no end is limited to damned souls!
Why wert thou not a creature wanting soul?
Or why is this immortal that thou hast?
Ah, Pythagoras' metempsychosis, were that true,
This soul should fly from me, and I be chang'd
Unto some brutish beast!174 all beasts are happy,
For, when they die,
Their souls are soon dissolv'd in elements;
But mine must live still to be plagu'd in hell.
Curs'd be the parents that engender'd me!
No, Faustus, curse thyself, curse Lucifer

That hath depriv'd thee of the joys of heaven.
    The clock strikes twelve.

O, it strikes, it strikes! Now, body, turn to air,
Or Lucifer will bear thee quick to hell!
    Thunder and lightning.

O soul, be chang'd into little water-drops,
And fall into the ocean, ne'er be found!
Enter DEVILS.
My God, my god, look not so fierce on me!
Adders and serpents, let me breathe a while!
Ugly hell, gape not! come not, Lucifer!
I'll burn my books!–Ah, Mephistophilis!
    eunt DEVILS with FAUSTUS.
175
Enter CHORUS.
CHORUS. Cut is the branch that might have grown full straight,
And burned is Apollo's laurel-bough,
That sometime grew within this learned man.
Faustus is gone: regard his hellish fall,
Whose fiendful fortune may exhort the wise,
Only to wonder at unlawful things,
Whose deepness doth entice such forward wits
To practice more than heavenly power permits.
    it.

Terminat hora diem; terminat auctor opus.

FOOTNOTES:

1
(return)
    mate– i.e. confound, defeat.

2
(return)
    vaunt– So the later 4tos.–2to 1604 "daunt."

3
(return)
    her– All the 4tos "his."

4
(return)
    Whereas– i.e. where.

5
(return)

cunning– i.e. knowledge.

6
(return)
So the later 4tos.–2to 1604 "more."

7
(return)
FAUSTUS discovered in his study– Most probably, the Chorus, before going out, drew a curtain, and discovered Faustus sitting. In B. Barnes's DIVILS CHARTER, 1607, we find; "SCEN. VLTIMA. ALEXANDER VNBRACED BETWIXT TWO CARDINALLS in his study LOOKING VPON A BOOKE, whilst a groome draweth the Curtaine." Sig. L 3.

8
(return)
Analytics, 'tis thou, c.– Qy. "Analytic"? (but such phraseology was not uncommon).

9
(return)
So the later 4tos.–2to 1604 "the" (the printer having mistaken "yt" for "ye").

10
(return)
So the later 4tos (with various spelling).–2to 1604 "Oncaymaeon."

11
(return)
and– So the later 4tos.–Not in 4to 1604.

12
(return)
Couldst– So the later 4tos.–2to 1604 "Wouldst."

13
(return)
men– So the later 4tos.–2to 1604 "man."

14
(return)
legatur– All the 4tos "legatus."

15
(return)
c.– So two of the later 4tos.–Not in 4to 1604.

16
(return)
  law– So the later 4tos.–2to 1604 "Church."

17
(return)
  This– So the later 4tos.–2to 1604 "His."

18
(return)
  Too servile– So the later 4tos.–2to 1604 "The deuill."

19
(return)
  Che sera, sera– Lest it should be thought that I am wrong in not altering the old spelling here, I may quote from Panizzi's very critical edition of the ORLANDO FURIOSO, "La satisfazion ci SERA pronta." C. xviii. st. 67.

20
(return)
  scenes– "And sooner may a gulling weather-spie By drawing forth heavens SCEANES tell certainly," c. Donne's FIRST SATYRE,–p. 327, ed. 1633.

21
(return)
  tire– So the later 4tos.–2to 1604 "trie."

22
(return)
  Enter WAGNER, c.– Perhaps the proper arrangement is,
"Wagner! Enter WAGNER. Commend me to my dearest friends," c.]
23
(return)
  treasure– So the later 4tos.–2to 1604 "treasury."

24
(return)
  Jove– So again, p. 84, first col.,[See Note 59
: "Seeing Faustus hath incurr'd eternal death By desperate thoughts against JOVE'S deity," c.: and I may notice that Marlowe is not singular in applying the name JOVE to the God of Christians:] "Beneath our standard of JOUES powerfull sonne [i.e. Christ–". MIR. FOR MAGISTRATES, p. 642, ed. 1610. "But see the judgement of almightie JOUE," c. Id. p. 696. "O sommo GIOVE per noi crocifisso," c. Pulci,–MORGANTE MAG. C. ii. st. 1.]
25
(return)

these elements– So again, "Within the bowels of THESE elements," c., p. 87, first col,[See Note 90—-"THESE" being equivalent to THE. (Not unfrequently in our old writers THESE is little more than redundant.)

26
(return)
　resolve– i.e. satisfy, inform.

27
(return)
　silk– All the 4tos "skill" (and so the modern editors!).

28
(return)
　the– So the later 4tos.–2to 1604 "our."

29
(return)
　the fiery keel at Antwerp's bridge– During the blockade of Antwerp by the Prince of Parma in 1585, "They of Antuerpe knowing that the bridge and the Stocadoes were finished, made a great shippe, to be a meanes to breake all this worke of the prince of Parmaes: this great shippe was made of masons worke within, in the manner of a vaulted caue: vpon the hatches there were layed myll-stones, graue-stones, and others of great weight; and within the vault were many barrels of powder, ouer the which there were holes, and in them they had put matches, hanging at a thred, the which burning vntill they came vnto the thred, would fall into the powder, and so blow vp all. And for that they could not haue any one in this shippe to conduct it, Lanckhaer, a sea captaine of the Hollanders, being then in Antuerpe, gaue them counsell to tye a great beame at the end of it, to make it to keepe a straight course in the middest of the streame. In this sort floated this shippe the fourth of Aprill, vntill that it came vnto the bridge; where (within a while after) the powder wrought his effect, with such violence, as the vessell, and all that was within it, and vpon it, flew in pieces, carrying away a part of the Stocado and of the bridge. The marquesse of Roubay Vicont of Gant, Gaspar of Robles lord of Billy, and the Seignior of Torchies, brother vnto the Seignior of Bours, with many others, were presently slaine; which were torne in pieces, and dispersed abroad, both vpon the land and vpon the water." Grimeston's GENERALL HISTORIE OF THE NETHERLANDS, p. 875, ed. 1609.

30
(return)
　only– Qy. "alone"? (This line is not in the later 4tos.)

31
(return)
　[Note ‖ from page 68 (The Second Part of Tamburlaine the Great):]

Vile– The 8vo "Vild"; the 4to "Wild" (Both eds. a little
before, have "VILE monster, born of some infernal hag", and,
a few lines after, "To VILE and ignominious servitude":–the
fact is, our early writers (or rather transcribers), with
their usual inconsistency of spelling, give now the one form,
and now the other: compare the folio SHAKESPEARE, 1623,
where we sometimes find "vild" and sometimes "VILE.")–]
    32
(return)
    concise syllogisms– Old ed. "Consissylogismes."

    33
(return)
    cunning– i.e. knowing, skilful.

    34
(return)
    Agrippa– i.e. Cornelius Agrippa.

    35
(return)
    shadow– So the later 4tos.–2to 1604 "shadowes."

    36
(return)
    irits– So the later 4tos.–2to 1604 "subiects."

    37
(return)
    Almain rutters– See note ***, p. 43.

[Note *** from p. 43. (The Second Part of Tamburlaine the
Great):
Almains, Rutters– Rutters are properly–German troopers
(reiter, reuter). In the third speech after the present one
this line is repeated VERBATIM: but in the first scene of
our author's FAUSTUS we have,
"Like ALMAIN RUTTERS with their horsemen's staves."–]
    38
(return)
    have the– So two of the later 4tos.–2to 1604 "in their."

    39
(return)
    From– So the later 4tos.–2to 1604 "For."

    40
(return)

– So the later 4tos.–Not in 4to 1604.

41
(return)
 renowm'd– See note ‖, p. 11.

[Note ‖ from p. 11. (The First Part of Tamburlaine the
Great):
renowmed– i.e. renowned.–So the 8vo.–The 4to "renowned."
–The form "RENOWMED" (Fr. RENOMME) occurs repeatedly
afterwards in this play, according to the 8vo. It is
occasionally found in writers posterior to Marlowe's
time. e.g.
"Of Constantines great towne RENOUM'D in vaine."
Verses to King James, prefixed to Lord Stirling's
MONARCHICKE TRAGEDIES, ed. 1607.–]
 42
(return)
 Albertus'– i.e. Albertus Magnus.–The correction of I. M. in Gent. Mag. for Jan.
1841.–All the 4tos "Albanus."

43
(return)
 cunning– i.e. skill.

44
(return)
 Enter two SCHOLARS– Scene, perhaps, supposed to be before Faustus's house,
as Wagner presently says, "My master is within at dinner."

45
(return)
 upon– So the later 4tos.–2to 1604 "vpon't."

46
(return)
 eak, would– So the later 4tos.–2to 1604 "speake, IT would."

47
(return)
 my dear brethren– This repetition (not found in the later 4tos) is perhaps an error
of the original compositor.

48
(return)

Enter FAUSTUS to conjure– The scene is supposed to be a grove; see p. 81, last line of sec. col. [Page 81, second column, last line: "VALDES. Then haste thee to some solitary grove,"–

49
(return)
    anagrammatiz'd– So the later 4tos.–2to 1604 "and Agramithist."

50
(return)
    Th' abbreviated– So the later 4tos.–2to 1604 "The breuiated."

51
(return)
    erring– i.e. wandering.

52
(return)
    surgat Mephistophilis, quod tumeraris– The later 4tos have "surgat Mephistophilis DRAGON, quod tumeraris."–There is a corruption here, which seems to defy emendation. For "quod TUMERARIS," Mr. J. Crossley, of Manchester, would read (rejecting the word "Dragon") "quod TU MANDARES" (the construction being "quod tu mandares ut Mephistophilis appareat et surgat"): but the "tu" does not agree with the preceding "vos."–The Revd. J. Mitford proposes "surgat Mephistophilis, per Dragon (or Dagon) quod NUMEN EST AERIS."

53
(return)
    dicatus– So two of the later 4tos.–2to 1604 "dicatis."

54
(return)
    Re-enter Mephistophilis, c.– According to THE HISTORY OF DR. FAUSTUS, on which this play is founded, Faustus raises Mephistophilis in "a thicke wood neere to Wittenberg, called in the German tongue Spisser Wolt..... Presently, not three fathom above his head, fell a flame in manner of a lightning, and changed itselfe into a globe..... Suddenly the globe opened, and sprung up in the height of a man; so burning a time, in the end it converted to the shape of a fiery man[?– This pleasant beast ran about the circle a great while, and, lastly, appeared in the manner of a Gray Fryer, asking Faustus what was his request?" Sigs. A 2, A 3, ed. 1648. Again; "After Doctor Faustus had made his promise to the devill, in the morning betimes he called the spirit before him, and commanded him that he should alwayes come to him like a fryer after the order of Saint Francis, with a bell in his hand like Saint Anthony, and to ring it once or twice before he appeared, that he might know of his certaine coming." Id. Sig. A 4.

55
(return)
    came hither– So two of the later 4tos.–2to 1604 "came NOW hither."

56
(return)
    accidens– So two of the later 4tos.–2to 1604 "accident."

57
(return)
    Why, this is hell, nor am I out of it– Compare Milton, Par. Lost, iv. 75; "Which way I fly is hell; myself am hell."

58
(return)
    these– So the later 4tos.–2to 1604 "those."

59
(return)
    Jove's– See note ****, p. 80. [i.e. Note 24
:]

60
(return)
    four and twenty– So the later 4tos.–2to 1604 "24."

61
(return)
    resolve– i.e. satisfy, inform.

62
(return)
    thorough– So one of the later 4tos.–2to 1604 "through."

63
(return)
    country– So the later 4tos.–2to 1604 "land."

64
(return)
    desir'd– So the later 4tos.–2to 1604 "desire."

65
(return)
    Enter WAGNER, c.– Scene, a street most probably.

66
(return)
    pickadevaunts– i.e. beards cut to a point.

67
(return)
   by'r lady– i.e. by our Lady.

68
(return)
   "Qui mihi discipulus, puer, es, cupis atque doceri,
Huc ades," c.]
   69
(return)
   staves-acre– A species of larkspur.

70
(return)
   vermin– Which the seeds of staves-acre were used to destroy.

71
(return)
   familiars– i.e. attendant-demons.

72
(return)
   their– So the later 4tos.–2to 1604 "my."

73
(return)
   slop– i.e. wide breeches.

74
(return)
   [Note ‖ from page 68 (The Second Part of Tamburlaine the
Great):
Vile– The 8vo "Vild"; the 4to "Wild" (Both eds. a little
before, have "VILE monster, born of some infernal hag", and,
a few lines after, "To VILE and ignominious servitude":–the
fact is, our early writers (or rather transcribers), with
their usual inconsistency of spelling, give now the one form,
and now the other: compare the folio SHAKESPEARE, 1623,
where we sometimes find "vild" and sometimes "VILE.")]
   75
(return)
   vestigiis nostris– All the 4tos "vestigias nostras."

76
(return)
   of– So the later 4tos.–Not in 4to 1604.

77
(return)
 me– So the later 4tos.–Not in 4to 1604.

78
(return)
 he lives– So the later 4tos.–2to 1604 "I liue."

79
(return)
 why– So the later 4tos.–Not in 4to 1604.

80
(return)
 Solamen miseris, c.– An often-cited line of modern Latin poetry: by whom it was written I know not.

81
(return)
 Why– So the later 4tos.–Not in 4to 1604.

82
(return)
 torture– So the later 4tos.–2to 1604 "tortures."

83
(return)
 Faustus– So the later 4tos.–Not in 4to 1604.

84
(return)
 Bill– i.e. writing, deed.

85
(return)
 Here's fire; come, Faustus, set it on– This would not be intelligible without the assistance of THE HISTORY OF DR. FAUSTUS, the sixth chapter of which is headed,–"How Doctor Faustus set his blood in a saucer on warme ashes, and writ as followeth." Sig. B, ed. 1648.

86
(return)
 But what is this inscription, c.– "He [Faustus– tooke a small penknife and prickt a veine in his left hand; and for certainty thereupon were seen on his hand these words written, as if they had been written with blood, O HOMO, FUGE." THE HISTORY OF DR. FAUSTUS, Sig. B, ed. 1648.

87
(return)
me– So the later 4tos.–2to 1604 "thee."

88
(return)
he desires– Not in any of the four 4tos. In the tract just cited, the "3d Article" stands thus,–"That Mephostophiles should bring him any thing, and doe for him whatsoever." Sig. A 4, ed. 1648. A later ed. adds "he desired." Marlowe, no doubt, followed some edition of the HISTORY in which these words, or something equivalent to them, had been omitted by mistake. (2to 1661, which I consider as of no authority, has "he requireth.")

89
(return)
that, c.– So all the 4tos, ungrammatically.

90
(return)
these– See note §, p. 80.[i.e. Note 25
:]
91
(return)
there– So the later 4tos.–Not in 4to 1604.

92
(return)
are– So two of the later 4tos.–2to 1604 "is."

93
(return)
fond– i.e. foolish.

94
(return)
What! walking, disputing, c.– The later 4tos have "What, SLEEPING, EATING, walking, AND disputing!" But it is evident that this speech is not given correctly in any of the old eds.

95
(return)
let me have a wife, c.– The ninth chapter of THE HISTORY OF DR. FAUSTUS narrates "How Doctor Faustus would have married, and how the Devill had almost killed him for it," and concludes as follows. "It is no jesting [said Mephistophilis– with us: hold thou that which thou hast vowed, and we will peforme as we have promised; and more shall that, thou shalt have thy hearts desire of what woman soever thou wilt, be she alive or dead, and so long as thou wilt thou shalt keep her by thee.–These words pleased Faustus wonderfull well, and repented himself that he was so foolish to wish

himselfe married, that might have any woman in the whole city brought him at his command; the which he practised and persevered in a long time." Sig. B 3, ed. 1648.

96
(return)
    me– Not in 4to 1604. (This line is wanting in the later 4tos.)

97
(return)
    no– So the later 4tos.–Not in 4to 1604.

98
(return)
    Saba– i.e. Sabaea–the Queen of Sheba.

99
(return)
    iterating– i.e. reciting, repeating.

100
(return)
    And argue of divine astrology, c.– In THE HISTORY OF DR. FAUSTUS, there are several tedious pages on the subject; but our dramatist, in the dialogue which follows, has no particular obligations to them.

101
(return)
    erring– i.e. wandering.

102
(return)
    freshmen's– "A Freshman, tiro, novitius." Coles's DICT. Properly, a student during his first term at the university.

103
(return)
    resolve– i.e. satisfy, inform.

104
(return)
    Seek to save– Qy. "Seek THOU to save"? But see note ‖, p. 18.

105
(return)
    Enter the SEVEN DEADLY SINS– In THE HISTORY OF DR. FAUSTUS, Lucifer amuses Faustus, not by calling up the Seven Deadly Sins, but by making various devils appear before him, "one after another, in forme as they were in hell." "First entered Beliall in forme of a beare," c.–"after him came Beelzebub, in curled haire of a

horseflesh colour," c.–"then came Astaroth, in the forme of a worme," c. c. During this exhibition, "Lucifer himselfe sate in manner of a man all hairy, but of browne colour, like a squirrell, curled, and his tayle turning upward on his backe as the squirrels use: I think he could crack nuts too like a squirrell." Sig. D, ed. 1648.

106
(return)
case– i.e. couple.

107
(return)
bevers– i.e. refreshments between meals.

108
(return)
L.– All the 4tos "Lechery."–Here I have made the alteration recommended by Mr. Collier in his Preface to COLERIDGE'S SEVEN LECTURES ON SHAKESPEARE AND MILTON, p. cviii.

109
(return)
LUCIFER. Away to hell, away! On, piper! [Exeunt the SINS.
FAUSTUS. O, how this sight doth delight my soul!" c.)]
110
(return)
I will send for thee at midnight– In THE HISTORY OF DR. FAUSTUS, we have a particular account of Faustus's visit to the infernal regions, Sig. D 2, ed. 1648.

111
(return)
Enter CHORUS– Old ed. "Enter WAGNER solus." That these lines belong to the Chorus would be evident enough, even if we had no assistance here from the later 4tos.–The parts of Wagner and of the Chorus were most probably played by the same actor: and hence the error.

112
(return)
Learned Faustus, To know the secrets of astronomy, c.– See the 21st chapter of THE HISTORY OF DR. FAUSTUS,–"How Doctor Faustus was carried through the ayre up to the heavens, to see the whole world, and how the sky and planets ruled," c.

113
(return)
Enter FAUSTUS and MEPHISTOPHILIS– Scene, the Pope's privy-chamber.

114
(return)

Trier– i.e. Treves or Triers.

115

(return)
From Paris next, c.– This description is from THE HISTORY OF DR. FAUSTUS; "He came from Paris to Mentz, where the river of Maine falls into the Rhine: notwithstanding he tarried not long there, but went into Campania, in the kingdome of Neapol, in which he saw an innumerable sort of cloysters, nunries, and churches, and great houses of stone, the streets faire and large, and straight forth from one end of the towne to the other as a line; and all the pavement of the city was of bricke, and the more it rained into the towne, the fairer the streets were: there saw he the tombe of Virgill, and the highway that he cu[t through the mighty hill of stone in one night, the whole length of an English mile," c. Sig. E 2, ed. 1648.]

116

(return)
The way he cut, c.– During the middle ages Virgil was regarded as a great magician, and much was written concerning his exploits in that capacity. The LYFE OF VIRGILIUS, however, (see Thoms's EARLY PROSE ROMANCES, vol. ii.,) makes no mention of the feat in question. But Petrarch speaks of it as follows. "Non longe a Puteolis Falernus collis attollitur, famoso palmite nobilis. Inter Falernum et mare mons est saxeus, hominum manibus confossus, quod vulgus insulsum a Virgilio magicis cantaminibus factum putant: ita clarorum fama hominum, non veris contenta laudibus, saepe etiam fabulis viam facit. De quo cum me olim Robertus regno clarus, sed praeclarus ingenio ac literis, quid sentirem, multis astantibus, percunctatus esset, humanitate fretus regia, qua non reges modo sed homines vicit, jocans nusquam me legisse magicarium fuisse Virgilium respondi: quod ille severissimae nutu frontis approbans, non illic magici sed ferri vestigia confessus est. Sunt autem fauces excavati montis angustae sed longissimae atque atrae: tenebrosa inter horrifica semper nox: publicum iter in medio, mirum et religioni proximum, belli quoque immolatum temporibus, sic vero populi vox est, et nullis unquam latrociniis attentatum, patet: Criptam Neapolitanam dicunt, cujus et in epistolis ad Lucilium Seneca mentionem fecit. Sub finem fusci tramitis, ubi primo videri coelum incipit, in aggere edito, ipsius Virgilii busta visuntur, pervetusti operis, unde haec forsan ab illo perforati montis fluxit opinio." ITINERARIUM SYRIACUM,–OPP. p. 560, ed. Bas.

117

(return)
From thence to Venice, Padua, and the rest, In one of which a sumptuous temple stands, c.– So the later 4tos.–2to 1604 "In MIDST of which," c.–THE HISTORY OF DR. FAUSTUS shews WHAT "sumptuous temple" is meant: "From thence he came to Venice....He wondred not a little at the fairenesse of S. Marks Place, and the sumptuous church standing thereon, called S. Marke, how all the pavement was set with coloured stones, and all the rood or loft of the church double gilded over." Sig. E 2, ed. 1648.

118

(return)
 Just through the midst, c.– This and the next line are not in 4to 1604. I have inserted them from the later 4tos, as being absolutely necessary for the sense.

119

(return)
 Ponte– All the 4tos "Ponto."

120

(return)
 of– So the later 4tos.–Not in 4to 1604.

121

(return)
 Then charm me, that I, c.– A corrupted passage.–Compare THE HISTORY OF DR. FAUSTUS, Sig. E 3, ed. 1648; where, however, the Cardinal, whom the Pope entertains, is called the Cardinal of PAVIA.

122

(return)
 Sonnet– Variously written, SENNET, SIGNET, SIGNATE, c.–A particular set of notes on the trumpet, or cornet, different from a flourish. See Nares's GLOSS. in V. SENNET.

123

(return)
 Enter ROBIN, c.– Scene, near an inn.

124

(return)
 ippocras– Or HIPPOCRAS,–a medicated drink composed of wine (usually red) with spices and sugar. It is generally supposed to have been so called from HIP-POCRATES (contracted by our earliest writers to HIPPOCRAS); perhaps because it was strained,–the woollen bag used by apothecaries to strain syrups and decoctions for clarification being termed HIPPOCRATES' SLEEVE.

125

(return)
 tabern– i.e. tavern.

126

(return)
 [Exeunt. Enter ROBIN and RALPH, c.– A scene is evidently wanting after the Exeunt of Robin and Ralph.

127

(return)

purchase– i.e. booty–gain, acquisition.

128

(return)
Drawer– There is an inconsistency here: the Vintner cannot properly be addressed as "Drawer." The later 4tos are also inconsistent in the corresponding passage: Dick says, "THE VINTNER'S BOY follows us at the hard heels," and immediately the "VINTNER" enters.

129

(return)
tone– i.e. the one.

130

(return)
MEPHIST– Monarch of hell, c.– Old ed. thus:–

"MEPHIST. Vanish vilaines, th' one like an Ape, an other like
a Beare, the third an Asse, for doing this enterprise.
Monarch of hell, vnder whose blacke suruey," c.
What follows, shews that the words which I have omitted ought to have no place in the text; nor is there any thing equivalent to them in the corresponding passage of the play as given in the later 4tos.]

131

(return)
Enter EMPEROR, c.– Scene–An apartment in the Emperor's Palace. According to THE HISTORY OF DR. FAUSTUS, the Emperor "was personally, with the rest of the nobles and gentlemen, at the towne of Inzbrack, where he kept his court." Sig. G, ed. 1648.

132

(return)
Master Doctor Faustus, c– The greater part of this scene is closely borrowed from the history just cited: e.g. "Faustus, I have heard much of thee, that thou art excellent in the black art, and none like thee in mine empire; for men say that thou hast a familiar spirit with thee, and that thou canst doe what thou list; it is therefore (said the Emperor) my request of thee, that thou let me see a proofe of thy experience: and I vow unto thee, by the honour of my emperiall crowne, none evill shall happen unto thee for so doing," c. Ibid.

133

(return)
won– May be right: but qy. "done"?

134

(return)

As we that do succeed, c.– A corrupted passage (not found in the later 4tos).

135
(return)
   The bright, c.– See note II, p. 18.

   [Note II, from page 18 (The First Part of Tamburlaine The
Great):
Barbarous– Qy. "O Barbarous"? in the next line but one,
"O treacherous"? and in the last line of the speech,
"O bloody"? But we occasionally find in our early dramatists
lines which are defective in the first syllable; and in
some of these instances at least it would almost seem that
nothing has been omitted by the transcriber or printer.–]
   136
(return)
   But, if it like your grace, it is not in my ability, c.
"D. Faustus answered, My most excellent lord, I am ready to accomplish your request
in all things, so farre forth as I and my spirit are able to performe: yet your majesty
shall know that their dead bodies are not able substantially to be brought before
you; but such spirits as have seene Alexander and his Paramour alive shall appeare
unto you, in manner and form as they both lived in their most flourishing time; and
herewith I hope to please your Imperiall Majesty. Then Faustus went a little aside to
speake to his spirit; but he returned againe presently, saying, Now, if it please your
Majesty, you shall see them; yet, upon this condition, that you demand no question
of them, nor speake unto them; which the Emperor agreed unto. Wherewith Doctor
Faustus opened the privy-chamber doore, where presently entered the great and mighty
emperor Alexander Magnus, in all things to looke upon as if he had beene alive; in
proportion, a strong set thicke man, of a middle stature, blacke haire, and that both
thicke and curled, head and beard, red cheekes, and a broad face, with eyes like a
basiliske; he had a compleat harnesse (i.e. suit of armour) burnished and graven,
exceeding rich to look upon: and so, passing towards the Emperor Carolus, he made
low and reverend courtesie: whereat the Emperour Carolus would have stood up to
receive and greet him with the like reverence; but Faustus tooke hold on him, and
would not permit him to doe it. Shortly after, Alexander made humble reverence, and
went out againe; and comming to the doore, his paramour met him. She comming
in made the Emperour likewise reverence: she was cloathed in blew velvet, wrought
and imbroidered with pearls and gold; she was also excellent faire, like milke and
blood mixed, tall and slender, with a face round as an apple. And thus passed [she–
certaine times up and downe the house; which the Emperor marking, said to himselfe,
Now have I seene two persons which my heart hath long wished to behold; and sure it
cannot otherwise be (said he to himselfe) but that the spirits have changed themselves
into these formes, and have but deceived me, calling to minde the woman that raised
the prophet Samuel: and for that the Emperor would be the more satisfied in the
matter, he said, I have often heard that behind, in her neck, she had a great wart or

wen; wherefore he tooke Faustus by the hand without any words, and went to see if it were also to be seene on her or not; but she, perceiving that he came to her, bowed downe her neck, when he saw a great wart; and hereupon she vanished, leaving the Emperor and the rest well contented." THE HISTORY OF DR. FAUSTUS, Sig. G, ed. 1648.]

137

(return)
   both– Old ed. "best."

138

(return)
   Mephistophilis, transform him straight– According to THE HISTORY OF DR. FAUSTUS, the knight was not present during Faustus's "conference" with the Emperor; nor did he offer the doctor any insult by doubting his skill in magic. We are there told that Faustus happening to see the knight asleep, "leaning out of a window of the great hall," fixed a huge pair of hart's horns on his head; "and, as the knight awaked, thinking to pull in his head, he hit his hornes against the glasse, that the panes thereof flew about his eares: thinke here how this good gentleman was vexed, for he could neither get backward nor forward." After the emperor and the courtiers, to their great amusement, had beheld the poor knight in this condition, Faustus removed the horns. When Faustus, having taken leave of the emperor, was a league and a half from the city, he was attacked in a wood by the knight and some of his companions: they were in armour, and mounted on fair palfreys; but the doctor quickly overcame them by turning all the bushes into horsemen, and "so charmed them, that every one, knight and other, for the space of a whole moneth, did weare a paire of goates hornes on their browes, and every palfry a paire of oxe hornes on his head; and this was their penance appointed by Faustus." A second attempt of the knight to revenge himself on Faustus proved equally unsuccessful. Sigs. G 2, I 3, ed. 1648.

139

(return)
   FAUSTUS. Now Mephistophilis, c.– Here the scene is supposed to be changed to the "fair and pleasant green" which Faustus presently mentions.

140

(return)
   Horse-courser– i.e. Horse-dealer.–We are now to suppose the scene to be near the home of Faustus, and presently that it is the interior of his house, for he falls asleep in his chair.–"How Doctor Faustus deceived a Horse-courser" is related in a short chapter (the 34th) of THE HISTORY OF DOCTOR FAUSTUS: "After this manner he served a horse-courser at a faire called Pheiffering," c.

141

(return)
   for forty– Qy. "for TWICE forty DOLLARS"?

142
(return)
　　to– So the later 4tos.–2to 1604 "vnto."

143
(return)
　　Doctor Lopus– i.e. Doctor Lopez, domestic physician to Queen Elizabeth, who was put to death for having received a bribe from the court of Spain to destroy her. He is frequently mentioned in our early dramas: see my note on Middleton's WORKS, iv. 384.

144
(return)
　　know of– The old ed. has "KNOWNE of"; which perhaps is right, meaning– acquainted with.

145
(return)
　　hey-pass– Equivalent to–juggler.

146
(return)
　　ostry– i.e. inn,–lodging.

147
(return)
　　cunning– i.e. skill.

148
(return)
　　"Exeunt.
Enter to them the DUKE, the DUTCHESS, the DUKE speakes."
In the later 4tos a scene intervenes between the "Exeunt" of Faustus, Mephistophilis, and Wagner, and the entrance of the Duke of Vanholt, c.–We are to suppose that Faustus is now at the court of the Duke of Vanholt: this is plain, not only from the later 4tos, –in which Wagner tells Faustus that the Duke "hath sent some of his men to attend him, with provision fit for his journey,"–but from THE HISTORY OF DOCTOR FAUSTUS, the subjoined portion of which is closely followed in the present scene. "Chap. xxxix. HOW DOCTOR FAUSTUS PLAYED A MERRY JEST WITH THE DUKE OF ANHOLT IN HIS COURT. Doctor Faustus on a time went to the Duke of Anholt, who welcommed him very courteously; this was the moneth of January; where sitting at the table, he perceived the dutchess to be with child; and forbearing himselfe untill the meat was taken from the table, and that they brought in the banqueting dishes [i.e. the dessert–, Doctor Faustus said to the dutchesse, Gratious lady, I have alwayes heard that great-bellied women doe alwayes long for some dainties; I beseech therefore your grace, hide not your minde from me, but tell me what you desire to eat. She answered him, Doctor Faustus, now truly I will not hide from you what my heart

doth most desire; namely, that, if it were now harvest, I would eat my bellyfull of grapes and other dainty fruit. Doctor Faustus answered hereupon, Gracious lady, this is a small thing for me to doe, for I can doe more than this. Wherefore he tooke a plate, and set open one of the casements of the window, holding it forth; where incontinent he had his dish full of all manner of fruit, as red and white grapes, peares, and apples, the which came from out of strange countries: all these he presented the dutchesse, saying, Madam, I pray you vouchsafe to taste of this dainty fruit, the which came from a farre countrey, for there the summer is not yet ended. The dutchesse thanked Faustus highly, and she fell to her fruit with full appetite. The Duke of Anholt notwithstanding could not withhold to ask Faustus with what reason there were such young fruit to be had at that time of the yeare. Doctor Faustus told him, May it please your grace to understand that the year is divided into two circles of the whole world, that when with us it is winter, in the contrary circle it is notwithstanding summer; for in India and Saba there falleth or setteth the sunne, so that it is so warm that they have twice a yeare fruit; and, gracious lord, I have a swift spirit, the which can in the twinkling of an eye fulfill my desire in any thing; wherefore I sent him into those countries, who hath brought this fruit as you see: whereat the duke was in great admiration."]

149

(return)
 Saba– i.e. Sabaea.

150

(return)
 beholding– i.e. beholden.

151

(return)
 Enter WAGNER– Scene, a room in the house of Faustus.

152

(return)
 he hath given to me all his goods– Compare chap. lvi. of THE HISTORY OF DOCTOR FAUSTUS,–"How Doctor Faustus made his will, in which he named his servant Wagner to be his heire."

153

(return)
 HELEN passeth over the stage– In THE HISTORY OF DOCTOR FAUSTUS we have the following description of Helen. "This lady appeared before them in a most rich gowne of purple velvet, costly imbrodered; her haire hanged downe loose, as faire as the beaten gold, and of such length that it reached downe to her hammes; having most amorous cole-black eyes, a sweet and pleasant round face, with lips as red as a cherry; her cheekes of a rose colour, her mouth small, her neck white like a swan; tall and slender of personage; in summe, there was no imperfect place in her: she looked round about with a rolling hawkes eye, a smiling and wanton countenance, which neere-hand inflamed the hearts of all the students; but that they perswaded themselves

she was a spirit, which made them lightly passe away such fancies." Sig. H 4, ed. 1648.

154
(return)
Enter an OLD MAN– See chap. xlviii of THE HISTORY OF DOCTOR FAUSTUS,– "How an old man, the neighbour of Faustus, sought to perswade him to amend his evil life and to fall into repentance," –according to which history, the Old Man's exhortation is delivered at his own house, whither he had invited Faustus to supper.

155
(return)
[Note ‖ from page 68 (The Second Part of Tamburlaine the Great):
Vile– The 8vo "Vild"; the 4to "Wild" (Both eds. a little before, have "VILE monster, born of some infernal hag", and, a few lines after, "To VILE and ignominious servitude":–the fact is, our early writers (or rather transcribers), with their usual inconsistency of spelling, give now the one form, and now the other: compare the folio SHAKESPEARE, 1623, where we sometimes find "vild" and sometimes "VILE.")–]
156
(return)
sin– Old ed. "sinnes" (This is not in the later 4tos).

157
(return)
almost– So the later 4tos.–Not in 4to 1604.

158
(return)
now– So the later 4tos.–Not in 4to 1604.

159
(return)
MEPHIST. Do it, then, quickly, c.– After this speech, most probably, there ought to be a stage-direction, "FAUSTUS STABS HIS ARM, AND WRITES ON A PAPER WITH HIS BLOOD. Compare THE HISTORY OF DOCTOR FAUSTUS, chap. xlix,– "How Doctor Faustus wrote the second time with his owne blood, and gave it to the Devill."

160
(return)
One thing, good servant, c.– "To the end that this miserable Faustus might fill the lust of his flesh and live in all manner of voluptuous pleasure, it came in his mind, after he had slept his first sleepe, and in the 23 year past of his time, that he had a great desire to lye with faire Helena of Greece, especially her whom he had seen and shewed

unto the students at Wittenberg: wherefore he called unto his spirit Mephostophiles, commanding him to bring to him the faire Helena; which he also did. Whereupon he fell in love with her, and made her his common concubine and bed-fellow; for she was so beautifull and delightfull a peece, that he could not be one houre from her, if he should therefore have suffered death, she had so stoln away his heart: and, to his seeming, in time she was with childe, whom Faustus named Justus Faustus. The childe told Doctor Faustus many things which were don in forraign countrys; but in the end, when Faustus lost his life, the mother and the childe vanished away both together." THE HISTORY OF DOCTOR FAUSTUS, Sig. I 4, ed. 1648.

161
(return)
    Those– So the later 4tos.–2to 1604 "These."

162
(return)
    Faustus, this– Qy. "This, Faustus"?

163
(return)
    topless– i.e. not exceeded in height by any.

164
(return)
    is– So the later 4tos.–2to 1604 "be."

165
(return)
    shalt– So all the 4tos; and so I believe Marlowe wrote, though the grammar requires "shall."

166
(return)
    Enter the OLD MAN– Scene, a room in the Old Man's house. –In THE HISTORY OF DOCTOR FAUSTUS the Old Man makes himself very merry with the attempts of the evil powers to hurt him. "About two dayes after that he had exhorted Faustus, as the poore man lay in his bed, suddenly there was a mighty rumbling in the chamber, the which he was never wont to heare, and he heard as it had beene the groaning of a sow, which lasted long: whereupon the good old man began to jest and mocke, and said, Oh, what a barbarian cry is this? Oh faire bird, what foul musicke is this? A[h–, faire angell, that could not tarry two dayes in his place! beginnest thou now to runne into a poore mans house, where thou hast no power, and wert not able to keepe thy owne two dayes? With these and such like words the spirit departed," c. Sig. I 2, ed. 1648.

167
(return)

Enter Faustus, c.– Scene, a room in the house of Faustus.

168
(return)
cunning– i.e. knowledge, skill.

169
(return)
Why did not Faustus tell us of this before, c.– "Wherefore one of them said unto him, Ah, friend Faustus, what have you done to conceale this matter so long from us? We would, by the helpe of good divines and the grace of God, have brought you out of this net, and have torne you out of the bondage and chaines of Satan; whereas now we feare it is too late, to the utter ruine both of your body and soule. Doctor Faustus answered, I durst never doe it, although I often minded to settle my life [myself?– to godly people to desire counsell and helpe; and once mine old neighbour counselled me that I should follow his learning and leave all my conjurations: yet, when I was minded to amend and to follow that good mans counsell, then came the Devill and would have had me away, as this night he is like to doe, and said, so soone as I turned againe to God, he would dispatch me altogether." THE HISTORY OF DOCTOR FAUSTUS, Sig. K 3, ed. 1648.

170
(return)
save– So the later 4tos.–Not in 4to 1604.

171
(return)
and what noise soever ye hear, c.– "Lastly, to knit up my troubled oration, this is my friendly request, that you would go to rest, and let nothing trouble you; also, if you chance heare any noyse or rumbling about the house, be not therewith afraid, for there shall no evill happen unto you," c. THE HISTORY OF DOCTOR FAUSTUS, ubi supra.

172
(return)
O lente, c. "At si, quem malles, Cephalum complexa teneres, Clamares, LENTE CURRITE, NOCTIS EQUI." Ovid,–AMOR. i. xiii. 39.

173
(return)
"That, when THEY vomit forth into the air,
My limbs may issue from THEIR smoky mouths," c.?]
174
(return)
and I be chang'd Unto some brutish beast– "Now, thou Faustus, damned wretch, how happy wert thou, if, as an unreasonable beast, thou mightest dye without [a–

soule! so shouldst thou not feele any more doubts," c. THE HISTORY OF DOCTOR FAUSTUS, Sig. K. ed. 1648.

175

(return)
eunt DEVILS with FAUSTUS– In THE HISTORY OF DOCTOR FAUSTUS, his "miserable and lamentable end" is described as follows: it took place, we are informed, at "the village called Rimlich, halfe a mile from Wittenberg."–"The students and the other that were there, when they had prayed for him, they wept, and so went forth; but Faustus tarried in the hall; and when the gentlemen were laid in bed, none of them could sleepe, for that they att[e–nded to heare if they might be privy of his end. It happened that betweene twelve and one a clocke at midnight, there blew a mighty storme of winde against the house, as though it would have blowne the foundation thereof out of his place. Hereupon the students began to feare and goe out of their beds, comforting one another; but they would not stirre out of the chamber; and the host of the house ran out of doores, thinking the house would fall. The students lay neere unto the hall wherein Doctor Faustus lay, and they heard a mighty noyse and hissing, as if the hall had beene full of snakes and adders. With that, the hall-doore flew open, wherein Doctor Faustus was, that he began to cry for helpe, saying, Murther, murther! but it came forth with halfe a voyce, hollowly: shortly after, they heard him no more. But when it was day, the students, that had taken no rest that night, arose and went into the hall, in the which they left Doctor Faustus; where notwithstanding they found not Faustus, but all the hall lay sprinkled with blood, his braines cleaving to the wall, for the devill had beaten him from one wall against another; in one corner lay his eyes, in another his teeth; a pittifull and fearefull sight to behold. Then began the students to waile and weepe for him, and sought for his body in many places. Lastly, they came into the yard, where they found his body lying on the horse-dung, most monstrously torne and fearefull to behold, for his head and all his joynts were dashed in peeces. The fore-named students and masters that were at his death, have obtained so much, that they buried him in the village where he was so grievously tormented. After the which they returned to Wittenberg; and comming into the house of Faustus, they found the servant of Faustus very sad, unto whom they opened all the matter, who tooke it exceeding heavily. There found they also this history of Doctor Faustus noted and of him written, as is before declared, all save only his end, the which was after by the students thereto annexed; further, what his servant had noted thereof, was made in another booke. And you have heard that he held by him in his life the spirit of faire Helena, the which had by him one sonne, the which he named Justus Faustus: even the same day of his death they vanished away, both mother and sonne. The house before was so darke that scarce any body could abide therein. The same night Doctor Faustus appeared unto his servant lively, and shewed unto him many secret things, the which he had done and hidden in his lifetime. Likewise there were certaine which saw Doctor Faustus looke out of the window by night, as they passed by the house." Sig. K 3, ed. 1648.

Original Comments on the preparation of the :

SQUARE BRACKETS:

The square brackets, i.e. [ ] are copied from the printed book, without change. The open [Exit brackets use in the book have been closed [by mh].

For this version of the book, the footnotes have been consolidated at the end of the play.

Numbering of the footnotes has been changed, and each footnote is given a unique identity in the form [XXX].

CHANGES TO THE TEXT:

Character names were expanded. For Example, SECOND SCHOLAR was SEC. SCHOL.